D1103904

Places In Time

A Kid's Historic Guide to the Changing Names and Places of the World

A Brief Political and Geographic History of

North America

P.O. Box 196
Hockessin, Delaware 19707
Visit us on the web: www.mitchelllane.com
Comments? email us: mitchelllane@mitchelllane.com

Places In Time

A Kid's Historic Guide to the Changing Names and Places of the World

Titles in the Series

A Brief Political and Geographic History of . . .

Africa

Where Are Belgian Congo, Rhodesia, and Kush?

Asia

Where Are Saigon, Kampuchea, and Burma?

Europe

Where Are Prussia, Gaul, and the Holy Roman Empire?

Latin America

Where Are Gran Columbia, La Plata, and Dutch Guiana?

The Middle East

Where Are Persia, Babylon, and the Ottoman Empire?

North America

Where Are New France, New Netherland, and New Sweden?

Places In Time

A Kid's Historic Guide to the Changing Names and Places of the World

A Brief Political and Geographic History of North America

Lissa Johnston

Mitchell Lane PUBLISHERS

P.O. Box 196
Hockessin, Delaware 19707
Visit us on the web: www.mitchelllane.com
Comments? email us: mitchelllane@mitchelllane.com

Printing 1 2 3 4 5 6 7 8 9

Library of Congress Cataloging-in-Publication Data
Johnston, Lissa Jones.
A brief political and geographic history of North America : where are New France, New Netherland, and New Sweden? / by Lissa Johnston.
p. cm. — (Places in time/a kid's historic guide to the changing names and places in the world)
Includes bibliographical references and index.
ISBN 978-1-58415-627-7 (library bound)
1. North America—History—Juvenile literature. 2. North America—Historical geography—Juvenile literature. I. Title.
E38.5.J64 2008
970—dc22

2007000798

PHOTO & MAP CREDITS: Maps by Jonathan Scott—pp. 6, 7, 16, 22, 26, 42, 48, 52, 57, 59, 72, 78; p. 8—Justus Danckerts, with Jonathan Scott; p. 11—Peter Schenk; pp. 12, 40, 75—Library of Congress; pp. 14, 18, 32, 34, 36, 74—North Wind Picture Archives; p. 19—Sharon Beck, with Jonathan Scott; pp. 21, 65, 66—National Archives of Canada; p. 28—Charles Willson Peale; p. 30—John Ogilby, Arnoldus Montanus, with Jonathan Scott; p. 35—Sharon Beck; p. 37—New-York Historical Society; p. 39—Peter Spier; p. 44—Axel Oxenstierna (unknown artist) and Queen Christina by Sébastien Bourdon; p. 45—Tim Kiser; p. 46—Swedish Colonial Society, Philadelphia; p. 54—John Mix Stanley; p. 56—Leonard Frank; p. 60—Library and Archives of Canada; p. 62—E Pluribus Anthony/Atlas of Canada; p. 64—Barbara Marvis; p. 67—Canadian Pacific Railway Archives; p. 68—Government of Nunavut; p. 69—National Library of Canada; p. 70—JupiterImages; p. 77—U.S. Army Center of Military History; p. 80—John Trumbull; p. 82—Golbez/Creative Commons; p. 84—Jacques-Louis David; p. 86—John William Hill; p. 88—Currier, N., lithographer. "City of Mexico. From the Convent of San Cosme." 1847. Prints and Photographs Division, Library of Congress; p. 91—Naval Historical Center; p. 92— National Atlas; p. 94—*New York Times*.

PUBLISHER'S NOTE: This story is based on the author's extensive research, which she believes to be accurate. Documentation of such research is contained on pages 104–106.

The maps created for these books have been thoroughly researched by our authors, who have extensive backgrounds in world history. Every effort has been made to represent close approximations to these places in time.

The internet sites referenced herein were active as of the publication date. Due to the fleeting nature of some web sites, we cannot guarantee they will all be active when you are reading this book.

To reflect current usage, we have chosen to use the secular era designations BCE ("before the common era") and CE ("of the common era") instead of the traditional designations BC ("before Christ") and AD (*anno Domini,* "in the year of the Lord").

PLB

Places In Time

Table of Contents

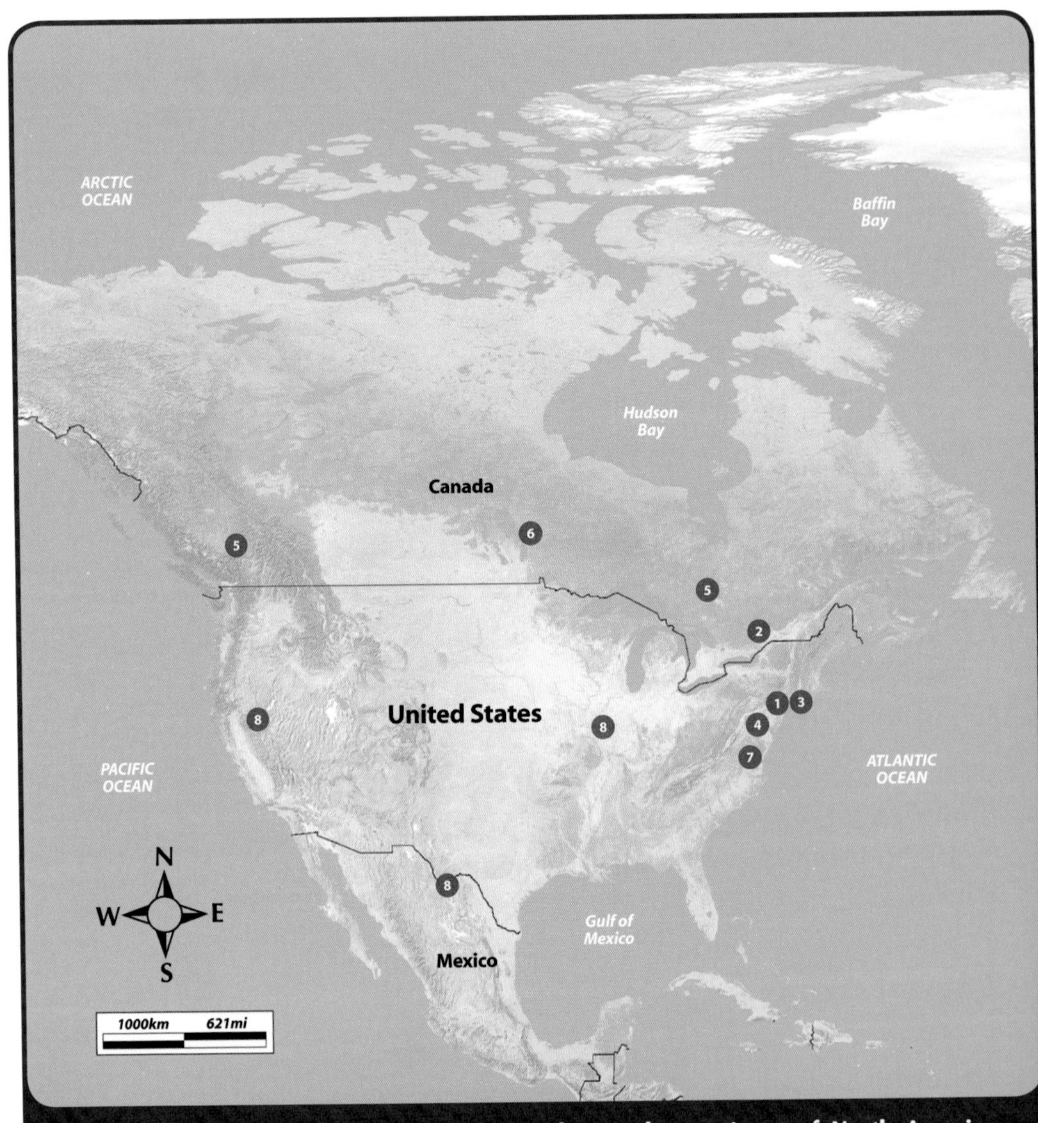

Canada, the United States, and Mexico make up the continent of North America. Throughout history, places in North America have changed names and boundaries several times. The numbers of the map indicate the chapters in which each area is discussed. More on Mexico can also be found in *A Brief Political and Geographic History of Latin America*, which is another book in the Places in Time series.

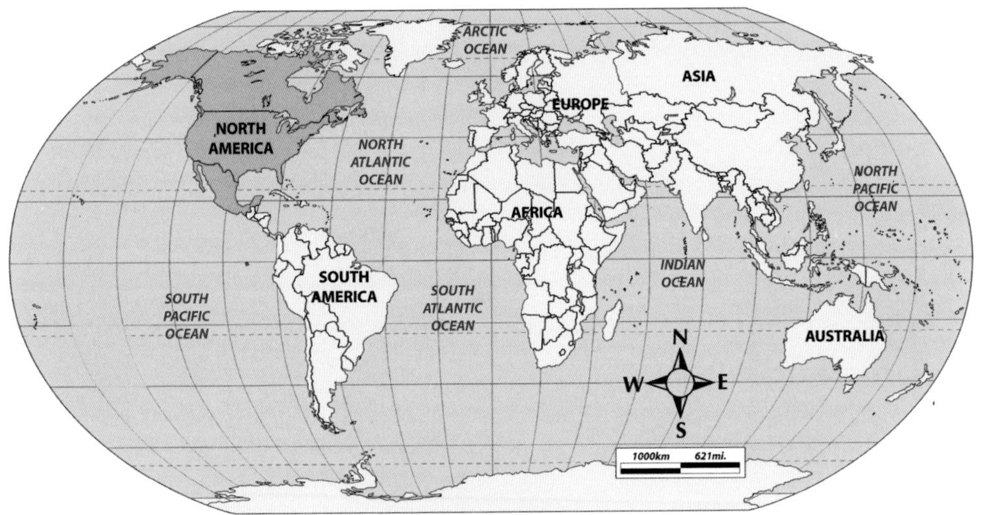

Introduction

Compare an old globe with a new one and you may be surprised to find some of the place names don't match up. No, it's not a printer's mistake. Sometimes places get new names. New people move to the place. New governments are put in charge. Sometimes they change the name. North America is one of these places that has had many names.

Early maps of the New World sometimes identified areas as "Terra Incognita," which means "unknown lands." On some maps, North America had no name at all. Of course, it had many names given by the native peoples already living there. But as Europeans moved in, they began renaming the areas they settled. Wars were fought, lands changed owners, and new names came yet again.

This book focuses on three colonies that played an important but little-known part in the history of North America. Their names are long gone, but simply changing the name of a place won't change its history. Clues to their existence are there, if you know where to look.

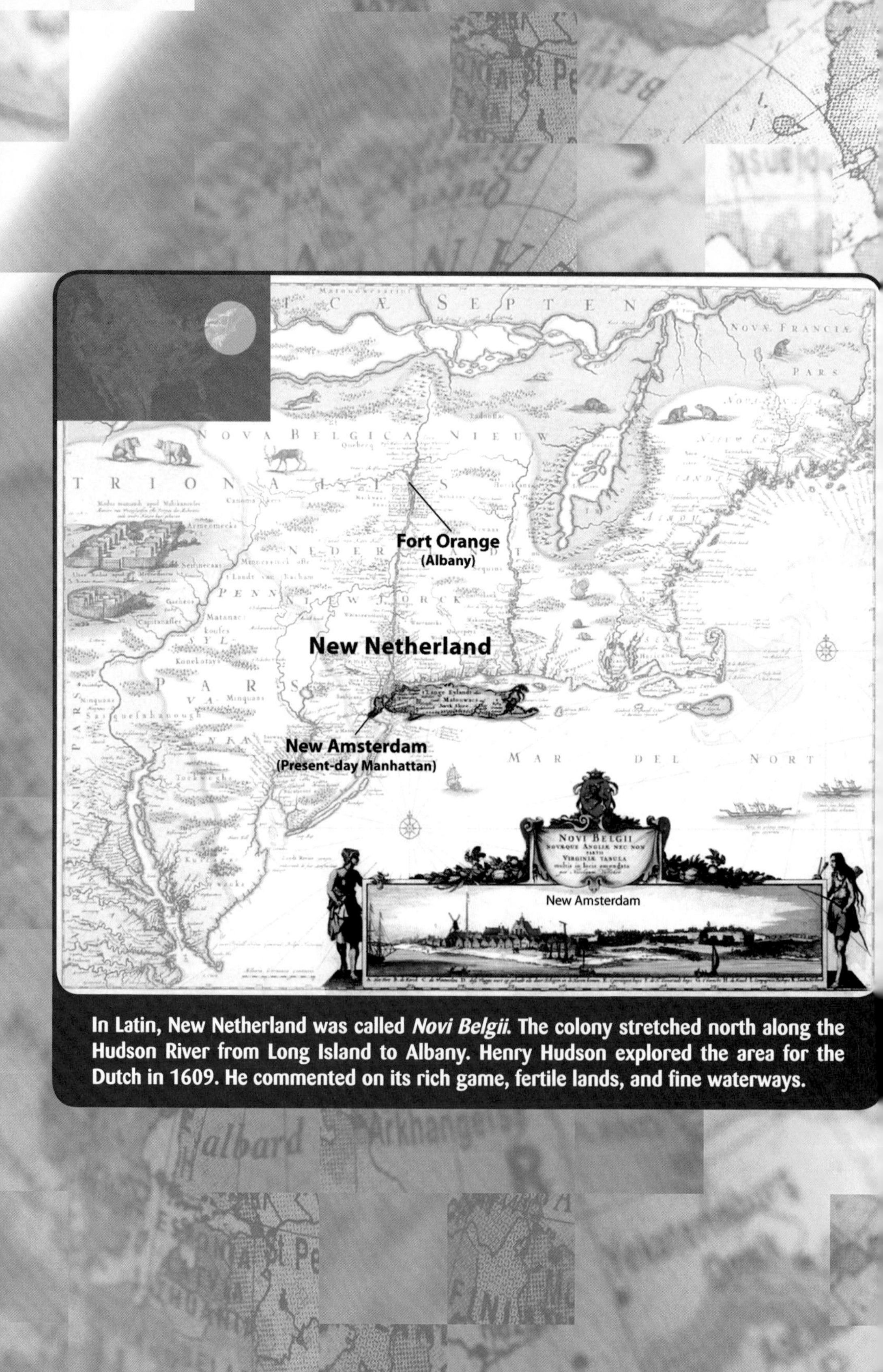

In Latin, New Netherland was called *Novi Belgii.* The colony stretched north along the Hudson River from Long Island to Albany. Henry Hudson explored the area for the Dutch in 1609. He commented on its rich game, fertile lands, and fine waterways.

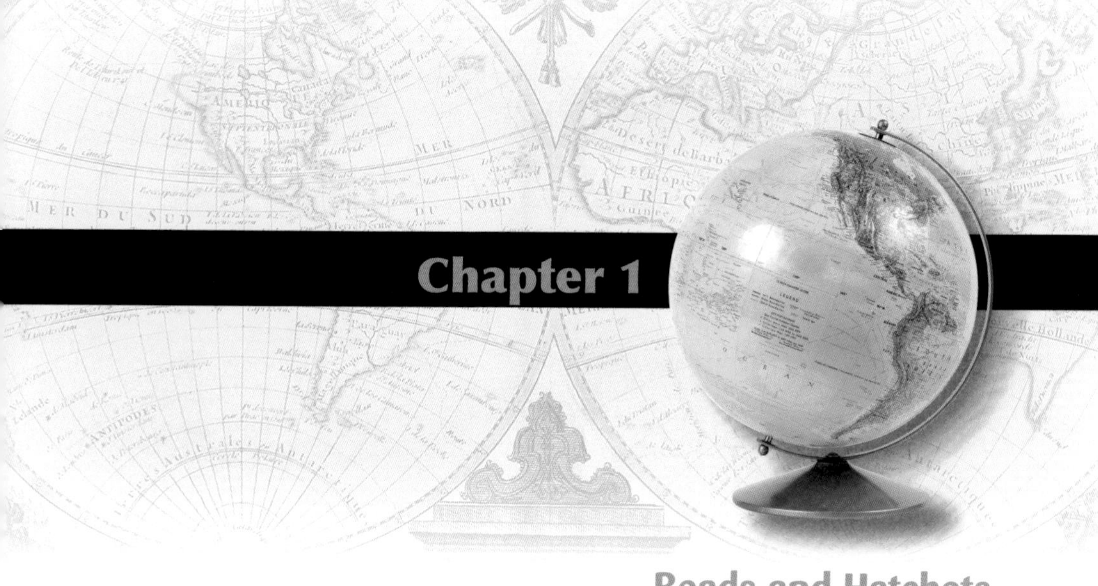

Chapter 1

Beads and Hatchets

In the spring of 1626, the little-known governor of a tiny Dutch colony bought Manhattan Island from a local clan of Lenape Indians. His name was Peter Minuit (pronounced min-WEE). He didn't buy the island with gold or hundred-dollar bills or money he had borrowed from a bank. Instead, he paid the Indians with trade goods. A Dutch official mentioned the sale in a letter to his superiors. He said that the value of these goods was about sixty guilders (a guilder is a unit of Dutch money). In the 1800s a scholar calculated that sixty guilders were worth about twenty-four dollars, based on currency values of his time. But no matter what the value, it was one of the most important real estate deals in history.[1]

Records of the transaction have been lost. We can only guess what actually happened, based on other land sales of the time. Minuit probably arranged a meeting with the leaders of the Indians living on *Manna-hata*, which in the local Indian language meant "hilly island." Perhaps Minuit invited the Indians to meet him near the proposed site of a Dutch fort on the southern tip of the island. The fort would protect the tiny Dutch settlement on Manhattan, which was called New Amsterdam. It was named for the Dutch city of Amsterdam.

Minuit probably brought some of his own men along. Perhaps he wanted to look important. Perhaps he also wanted to have some protection in case something went wrong. Any interested settlers may have gathered around and witnessed history in the making. There weren't many buildings in Manhattan then—just rolling hills in the

WILLEM II KONING DER NED. G.H.V.L.

1848. MUNT VAN HET KONINGRIJK DER NEDERLANDEN.
1 G

Dutch guilders were one of many types of money used in New Netherland. Spanish doubloons and pieces of eight, English pennies and pounds, and even animal furs were exchanged for goods. Wampum, beads made from shells, was by far the most common currency.

distance, reedy marshes bordering the nearby harbor, and seabirds calling overhead.[2]

Often the Europeans would have some papers drawn up to describe the land they were buying. They would sign the papers and ask the Indians to do the same. The Indians couldn't read or write, so they woud make a simple mark on the paper to show they agreed.

This transaction has been viewed with scorn. Some people think the Indians were foolish to sell Manhattan for such a small amount. But from the natives' viewpoint, this was not a sale of their land. The Indians did not have a concept of land ownership. They believed the land, water, and air belonged to everyone equally. In their minds, the transaction was more of an agreement between two peoples. By

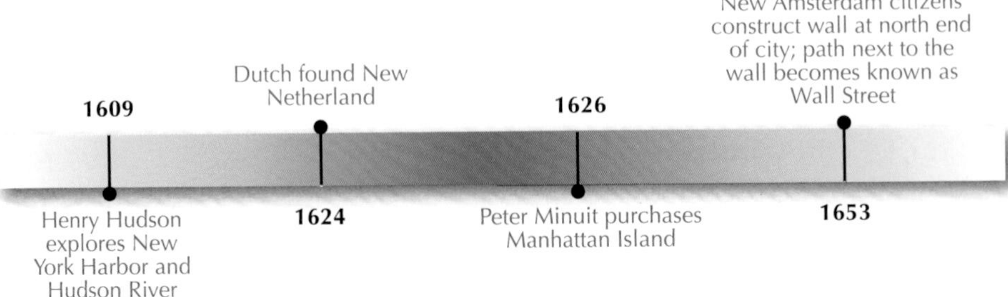
1609
Henry Hudson explores New York Harbor and Hudson River
1624
Dutch found New Netherland
1626
Peter Minuit purchases Manhattan Island
1653
New Amsterdam citizens construct wall at north end of city; path next to the wall becomes known as Wall Street

accepting a handful of trinkets from the Dutch, the natives agreed to share hunting and trading rights. They also expected the Dutch to work together with them both in peacetime and when at war.[3]

We don't know exactly what Minuit traded for Manhattan. The Indians were very fond of metal items such as knives, hatchets, and cooking pots. Before the Europeans came, the Indians had not discovered how to make metal.[4]

New Amsterdam began as a cluster of modest buildings on the southern tip of Manhattan Island. It resembled its namesake city with its busy harbor, docks, and even a few windmills. New Amsterdam was renamed New York City in 1665.

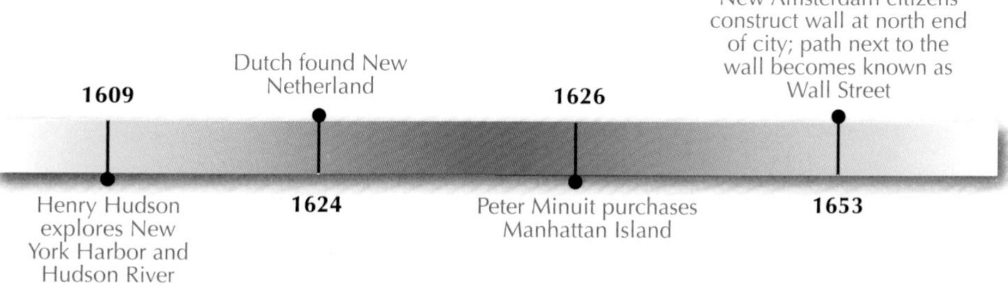
1609
Henry Hudson explores New York Harbor and Hudson River
1624
Dutch found New Netherland
1626
Peter Minuit purchases Manhattan Island
1653
New Amsterdam citizens construct wall at north end of city; path next to the wall becomes known as Wall Street

Other types of trade goods may also have been a part of this transaction. The Europeans often traded beads for decorating clothing, guns and gunpowder, or even alcohol. The Indians also liked the woven cloth the Europeans brought because they had no way of weaving their own. They made their clothing from animal skins.

The Dutchmen and the Indians could not have been more different. The Indians may have worn deerskin leggings or even only a breechcloth, probably no shirt. Their faces were clean shaven. The younger men shaved everything except for a small bit on the top of their head, decorated with a few feathers. Perhaps they had colored themselves with red, white, black, or yellow paint on this special occasion. No doubt they sported a few tattoos. The chief, if he was older, may have had very long hair. He may have worn an intricately designed wampum belt.[5]*

The Dutch likely were clothed in the tradition of their homeland. It was simple, practical clothing—knee-length pants over boots, and a shirt complete with long, full sleeves, tucked into a wide leather belt. Perhaps they had some facial hair, which was in fashion at the time—long pointed mustaches and chin beards to match. We don't know what their hair looked like. It was likely covered by a tall, floppy-brimmed beaver hat (which was part of the reason they were all gathered around in the first place).†

The purchase of Manhattan Island wouldn't have taken long. Neither side understood the language of the other very well yet. Some big

*See page 15
†See page 29

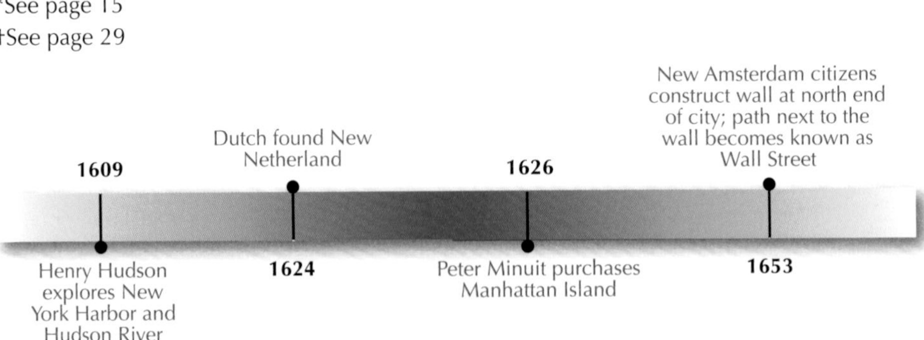
1609
Henry Hudson explores New York Harbor and Hudson River
Dutch found New Netherland
1624
1626
Peter Minuit purchases Manhattan Island
New Amsterdam citizens construct wall at north end of city; path next to the wall becomes known as Wall Street
1653

pronouncements, much gesturing, the giving of the trade goods, and the signing of the papers would have completed the transaction. Manhattan Island now belonged to the Dutch.

The Dutch had a single purpose: to make money. They were businessmen, tradesmen. Their colonies were geared toward turning a profit. In New Netherland, this would be accomplished by entering the fur trade.

Those coming after, though not always Dutch, often had the same purpose. The sale of Manhattan signified the coming of a new civilization. The arrival of the Europeans would change everything. The forests teeming with game would someday be replaced by towering

Wampum belts consisted of thousands of small beads strung together. The beads were made by hand by the local Indians until Europeans arrived with better tools. Purple beads like those shown in this belt were twice as valuable as white beads.

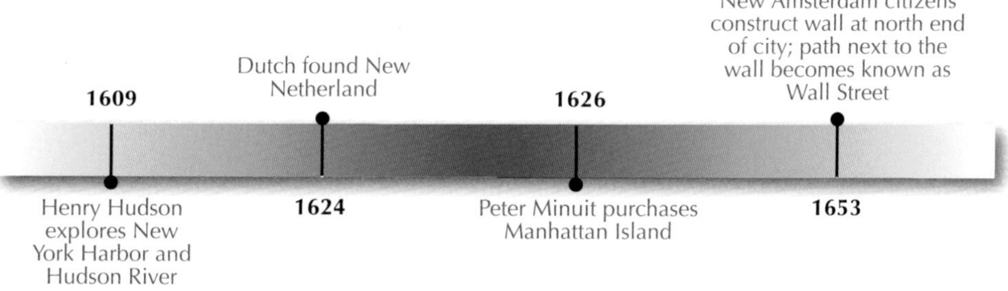
1609
Henry Hudson explores New York Harbor and Hudson River
1624
Dutch found New Netherland
1626
Peter Minuit purchases Manhattan Island
1653
New Amsterdam citizens construct wall at north end of city; path next to the wall becomes known as Wall Street

Increasing conflicts with the British led Dutch colonists to build a wall across the northern end of their settlement on Manhattan Island. Although the wall was torn down soon after its construction, its namesake lives on as the famous Wall Street.

skyscrapers. In place of the flocks of migrating geese and swans would be crowds of people rushing on foot, in cars, in taxis, on bicycles, and on subways. Trading of beads and metal axes would be replaced by multimillion-dollar business transactions taking place on Wall Street. Once a pristine wilderness, Manhattan would become one of the greatest financial centers in the world.

Wampum

When Europeans arrived in the New World, they wanted to be prepared with trade goods in case they found gold, silver, spices, or furs. They brought large quantities of trade items such as glass beads, woven cloth, metal tools, and pots, which were very popular with the Indians. The Indians did not have the technology to make these things and quickly grew fond of them. They would willingly give up their riches to the Europeans for these goods.

Almost by accident, Dutch trader Isaac de Rasieres discovered something else the Indians were willing to trade for. It was *wampumpeake*, which meant "white beads." This native word was often shortened to *wampum*. Wampum consisted of round beads made from shells. The beads were strung together in a variety of lengths. Some were woven together to make belts or bracelets. Wampum was difficult to make. The shells had to be shaped and drilled by hand. The strands were valued for the time it took to make them, as well as for the different designs that could be made with them.[6]

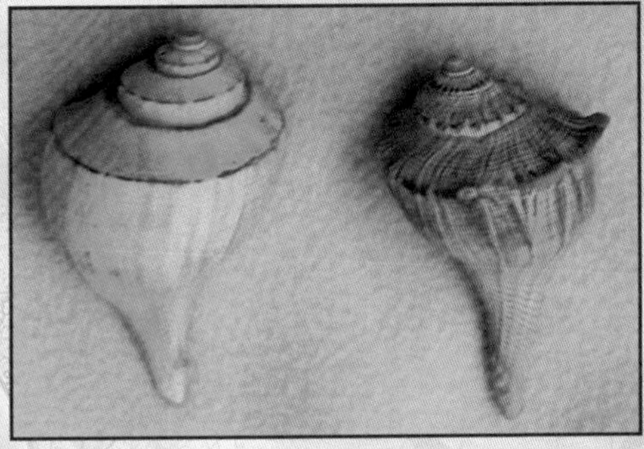

Whelk shells

The Indians used a variety of shells to make wampum. For white wampum beads, they used whelk shells. The more valuable purple beads came from the inner chambers of quahog shells. The drilled shells were shaped by rubbing them with sand. Then they were strung together with sinew or twine.[7]

Quahog shell

The most common form of wampum was a strand about six feet long, or a *fathom*. A fathom of white beads was worth about ten shillings (about one dollar at that time). The purple beads were worth twice that amount.[8]

To the Indians, wampum was never a form of money. It was a symbol of an important event or an agreement, similar to a wedding ring or a sports trophy. The Europeans may not have understood this. But they knew wampum was as good or better than any other item they had to trade, and they used it extensively. Wampum was still in use up until the time of the American Revolution.[9]

For Your Information

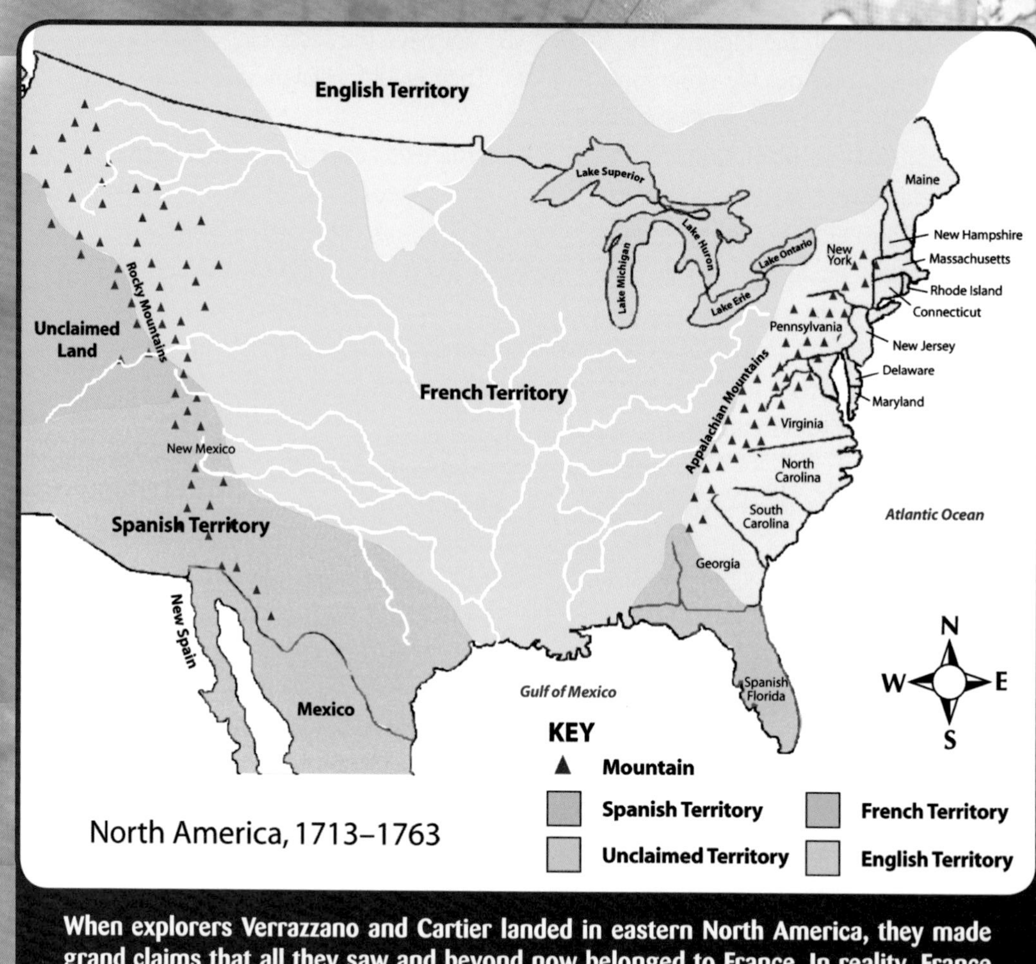

North America, 1713–1763

When explorers Verrazzano and Cartier landed in eastern North America, they made grand claims that all they saw and beyond now belonged to France. In reality, France controlled only the areas bordering the St. Lawrence River from the Atlantic Ocean to the Great Lakes. Eventually their territory also included all rivers (and associated lands) flowing into the Mississippi River.

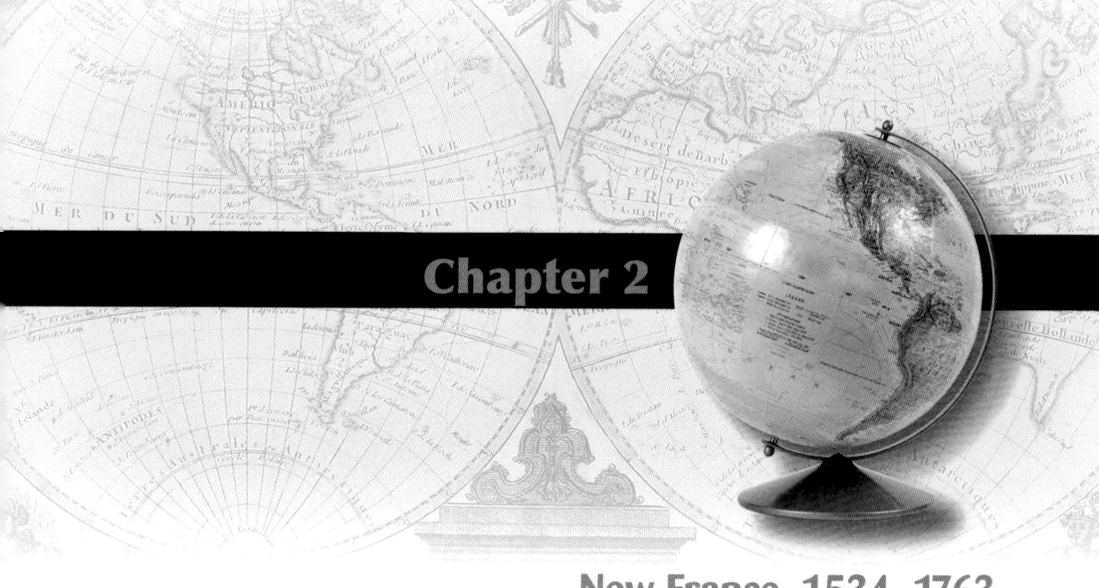

Chapter 2

New France, 1534–1763

After the discovery of the New World by Christopher Columbus in 1492, Spain wasted no time exploring and claiming its lands. Columbus's discovery resulted in a wealth of gold and silver delivered to the Old World. But his voyage had not solved the greatest puzzle of the time: finding a western route to Asia. Trade goods from Asia, especially spices like pepper and cinnamon, were more popular than ever. Europeans had to follow a complicated route to obtain them. The cost of bringing them to Europe had risen dramatically in the 1400s.[1]

In an effort to reduce this cost, Portuguese navigators had established the likelihood of a direct sea route to the east around the southern tip of Africa. Geographers of the time believed that an even shorter route could be found by sailing west instead of east. This belief spurred Columbus to undertake his famous voyage.

In 1519, Ferdinand Magellan set out from Spain to try to find the same western route that Columbus had sought. When his one surviving ship returned in 1521 after sailing around the world, it proved there was no shortcut to Asia around South America. European powers turned their attention to the possibilities of a route through or around North America. The French were among the leaders in this effort. French fishermen had long known of the rich schools of cod off the coast of Labrador. In 1524 France made its move to stake a claim in the lands across the Atlantic.[2]

King Francis I of France sent Italian explorer Giovanni da Verrazzano to the New World to seek the western route. Verrazzano explored the North American coast from the Carolinas to Maine. Although he did not find a route to China, he did claim all that he saw for France. The term *Gallia Nova* (New France) first appeared on a map in 1529.[3]

The king remained determined to find a western route to China. He sent Jacques Cartier, an experienced sea captain, to the New World in 1534. When he landed at the Gaspé Peninsula, Cartier erected a large cross to reinforce France's claim. He met with the local Indians. They told him the name of their village: *kanata*. Cartier misunderstood and thought that was their name for the entire region.[4] "Canada" would become the country's name centuries later.

Jacques Cartier erects a cross at Gaspé Peninsula, claiming the lands for France. The peninsula borders the St. Lawrence River where it empties into the Gulf of St. Lawrence.

Cartier continued exploring the coastline, then sailed up the St. Lawrence River (which he named) to Montreal. But he could go no further because of a series of rapids he encountered there.

In all, Cartier made three voyages. Try as he might, his attempts to found a French outpost failed. He had mixed success with the Indians. The first contacts were friendly, but did not remain so. Con-

1492
Christopher Columbus sails to the Americas
1519
Ferdinand Magellan sets out to sail around the world
1524
Giovanni da Verrazzano explores North American coast for France
1529
Gallia Nova (New France) first appears on a map of North America
1534
Jacques Cartier claims New France for King Francis I

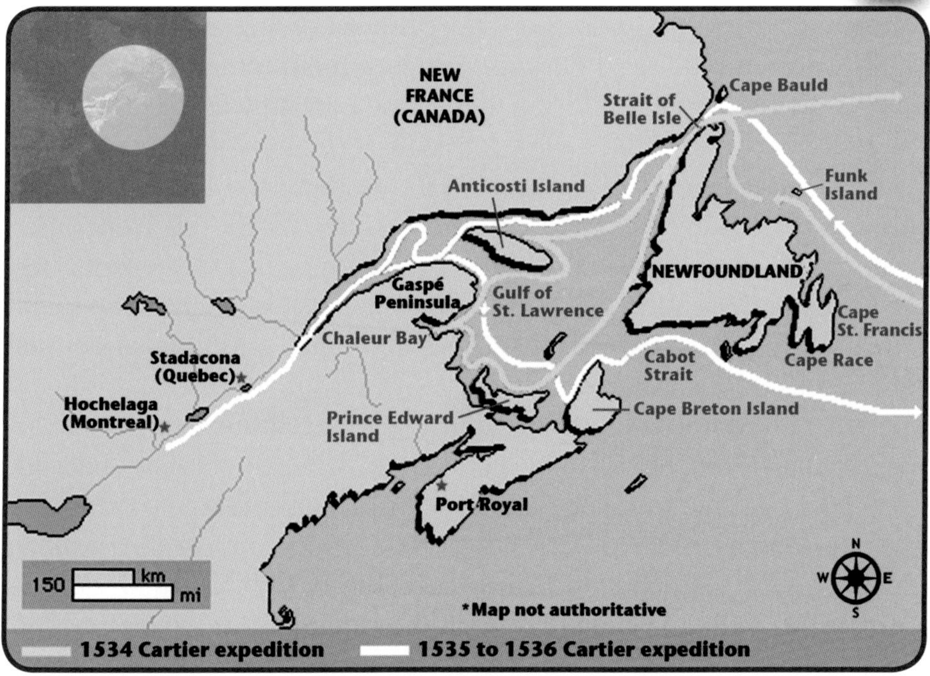

Jacques Cartier explored the waters of eastern Canada extensively. He named the St. Lawrence River and sailed it as far as the rapids at Montreal.

flict erupted; many died. The winters were very harsh and more men died. Cartier's main goal, to find a route to China, was unsuccessful. He found no gold, no silver, no spices. The diamonds he thought he found turned out to be common quartz. Cartier returned to France in 1542 and the surviving settlers came with him. New France sat virtually abandoned.[5]

Although the French monarchy had given up interest in New France, the French fishermen had not. They continued to fish the

waters off the coast. Some spent time ashore drying and salting their catch before returning to Europe. A few of them remained behind to protect the best locations. Soon they made contact with the Indians in the area.[6]

The Indians were very interested in the items the Frenchmen had to trade, especially metal knives and cooking tools. The Frenchmen were equally interested in the natives' animal pelts, or furs—especially beaver pelts. They soon discovered they could trade a few cheap metal knives for highly valuable beaver pelts and make a fortune when they returned to France.[7]

Why a fortune? Because the rich, thick beaver fur was perfect for making hats: hats for wealthy gentlemen, hats for soldiers, hats for men, women, children. Felt hats made from beaver fur were extremely popular. When New World beaver pelts began to appear in European seaports, they commanded high prices. The French found no gold in Canada, no route to China, but the furs made up for these failures.[8]

The increasing number of beaver furs coming from Canada helped rekindle interest in New France during the reign of Henry IV, who became king in 1589. He ordered an expedition to reestablish a French presence on the St. Lawrence River. Leading this expedition were Samuel de Champlain and Pierre du Gua, sieur de Monts. Their goals remained to seek wealth and a route to China. By this time they also knew codfish and pelts could provide a steady income.[9]

Champlain and de Monts did little better than Cartier. In 1605, they founded the first French settlement in North America, Port Royal. The settlement didn't do well. Many men died from the cold, hunger, and scurvy. The Indians were hostile. In 1607 the survivors returned to France.

1492
Christopher Columbus sails to the Americas
1519
Ferdinand Magellan sets out to sail around the world
1524
Giovanni da Verrazzano explores North American coast for France
1529
Gallia Nova (New France) first appears on a map of North America
1534
Jacques Cartier claims New France for King Francis I

But Champlain was not ready to quit. In 1608 he returned with a new group of settlers. He felt a settlement farther up the St. Lawrence would be more successful. He chose a site near a massive rocky outcropping a hundred miles upstream and founded Quebec.[10]

The location of Quebec was excellent. Backed up against the rock face, it was easy to defend. It was much closer to the Indian fur traders. Champlain was pleased with the site and began work on the construction of a wooden stockade and other buildings. He and his men would need all the shelter they could get when winter arrived.

Hats made from beaver felt were in fashion for hundreds of years. They came in all shapes and sizes. The toxic chemical mercury was used to make felt from the beaver pelt. Mercury caused a range of illnesses among hat makers, or "hatters."

Quebec's location was important to the success of the French fur trade. So were the Indians. The Indians were in control of the fur trade. They were very smart businessmen. They were the only ones who knew the backcountry trails.

Over time, many Frenchmen joined the Indians in hunting and trading beaver. Eventually they became almost as familiar with the

1542
French colony fails but fur trade initiated
Henry IV becomes king of France
1589
1603
Samuel de Champlain sails up St. Lawrence River
Champlain founds Quebec
1608
1627
Cardinal Richelieu founds Company of New France

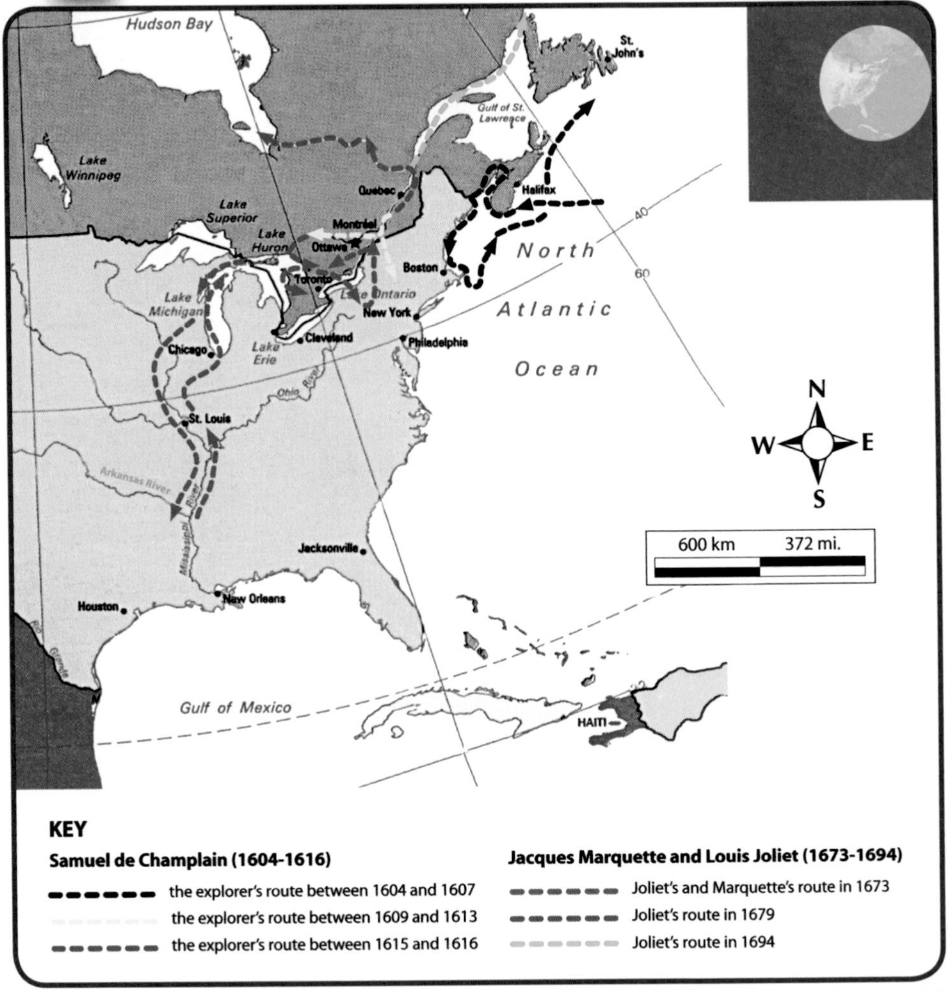

KEY

Samuel de Champlain (1604-1616)

- the explorer's route between 1604 and 1607
- the explorer's route between 1609 and 1613
- the explorer's route between 1615 and 1616

Jacques Marquette and Louis Joliet (1673-1694)

- Joliet's and Marquette's route in 1673
- Joliet's route in 1679
- Joliet's route in 1694

French explorer Robert de La Salle achieved what French explorers before him could not. He followed the Mississippi to its mouth at the Gulf of Mexico in 1682. La Salle later attempted to find the Mississippi by sea. He overshot it and landed near present-day Galveston, Texas, instead.

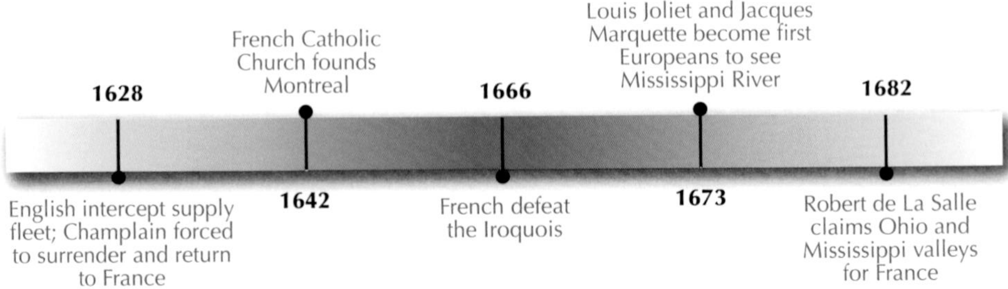
1628
English intercept supply fleet; Champlain forced to surrender and return to France
1642
French Catholic Church founds Montreal
1666
French defeat the Iroquois
1673
Louis Joliet and Jacques Marquette become first Europeans to see Mississippi River
1682
Robert de La Salle claims Ohio and Mississippi valleys for France

country as the Indians themselves. They were known as coureurs de bois ("woodsmen") or voyageurs ("travelers"). These men played an important role in the expansion of New France.

The French, starting with Champlain, understood the importance of a good relationship with their Indian trading partners, the Algonquins and the Hurons. If they wanted to keep trading, the French knew the Indians had certain expectations. They wanted good prices for their pelts. They also expected the French to fight with them in times of war with their enemies, the Iroquois. The French did so in order to keep the beaver trade healthy.[11]

Though they had fewer men, the French were better armed than the Indians. But they soon discovered having guns did not necessarily guarantee victory. The Indians did not fight according to European rules. They did not arrange a battle at a certain time and place. They did not face the French across open fields. They did not line up in neat lines and fire their weapons all at the same time.

Instead, they freely roamed the thick Canadian forests. They used the landscape to hide their movements. The French never knew when or where the Iroquois and their allies would attack. Sometimes there were only a handful of Indians. Sometimes there were hundreds.

Champlain knew a military force was just as important to holding the settlement as an infusion of permanent settlers. He pleaded for more support from France. But troubles at home—succession issues, a religious war—kept the French colony low on the list of priorities of King Louis XIII, who had succeeded Henry IV in 1610.

The king's chief minister, Cardinal Richelieu, renewed royal support of New France. In 1627 he organized a company of more than one hundred investors to support the colony. He arranged to send more

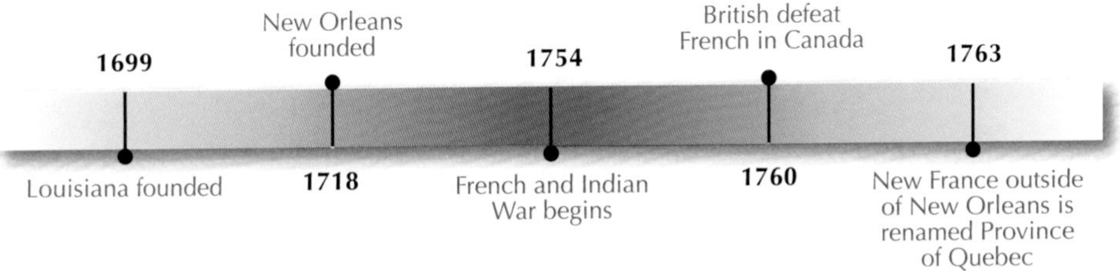
1699
Louisiana founded
New Orleans founded
1718
1754
French and Indian War begins
British defeat French in Canada
1760
1763
New France outside of New Orleans is renamed Province of Quebec

settlers and supplies to New France. But as the first ships carrying 400 settlers sailed, England and France declared war. The ships were intercepted by the English before they reached Quebec. Starving and undermanned, Quebec surrendered to the British, though the settlement was soon returned to France as part of a peace treaty.[12]

The loss of the supply ships was the end of the investing Company of One Hundred Associates. No more money was available from the French government, but individual investors were still willing to bet on Canada. Slowly but surely the population increased, towns grew, farms prospered.[13]

In 1642, a group of religious colonists founded a settlement on the island of Montreal. Montreal was even farther up the St. Lawrence from Quebec. At first the purpose of the settlement was to aid and convert the Indian population to the Christian religion. With its prime location at the intersection of the St. Lawrence and Ottawa Rivers, it soon became a trading center as well.

Problems with the Iroquois remained. In 1665, more than 1,000 French troops marched against them. Soon afterward, the Iroquois agreed to sign a peace treaty. With the threat of Indian attacks removed, the colony could move forward. Agriculture improved, making the colony more self-sufficient. Every summer ships brought more colonists, building supplies, and livestock. Many soldiers remained in New France after their tour of duty was over. At last the population was able to sustain itself and indeed multiply.

The boundaries of New France expanded as the French voyageurs and explorers pushed farther south and west. They learned about distant lands from the Indians. The colony sent men to explore these lands.

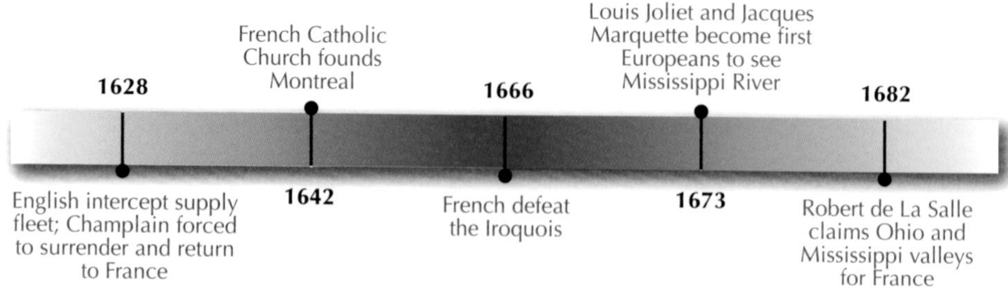
1628
English intercept supply fleet; Champlain forced to surrender and return to France
1642
French Catholic Church founds Montreal
1666
French defeat the Iroquois
1673
Louis Joliet and Jacques Marquette become first Europeans to see Mississippi River
1682
Robert de La Salle claims Ohio and Mississippi valleys for France

The quest for a western route to Asia had not been forgotten. The French heard many tales of a great river leading to the "Southern Sea" that they figured separated New France from China. They still hoped one of the great rivers in the land would be the key.

Champlain had explored various waterways west as far as Lake Huron. He also sent a young man named Jean Nicollet to live with the Algonquins. Nicollet spent more than ten years among the Indians and learned to speak their languages. Beginning in 1634 he journeyed along the western shore of Lake Michigan to Green Bay, then down the Fox River into Wisconsin. But he didn't find the great river.

Several decades later, Louis Joliet and Father Jacques Marquette were more successful. They also traveled through Wisconsin. The Wisconsin River led them to the great river—the Mississippi—in June, 1673. They were the first Frenchmen to see it. What a sight it must have been—another vast river every bit as broad and powerful as the St. Lawrence. They traveled down the Mississippi to the Arkansas River before being turned back by hostile Indians.

Robert de La Salle continued their efforts and in 1682 reached the mouth of the Mississippi. He claimed the river and all lands draining into it for France. He named the region Louisiana in honor of his king, Louis XIV, who ruled France from 1643 to 1715.[14]

New France now covered millions of square miles. It stretched from the Atlantic Ocean in northeast Canada to the Gulf of Mexico. But there was a problem. With a population of only ten thousand people, how could the French hold on to so much territory?[15] England, Spain, and the Netherlands also wanted a bigger share of the New World trade. The French did not have enough colonists to create new settlements. Instead, they built forts along rivers and lakes to protect

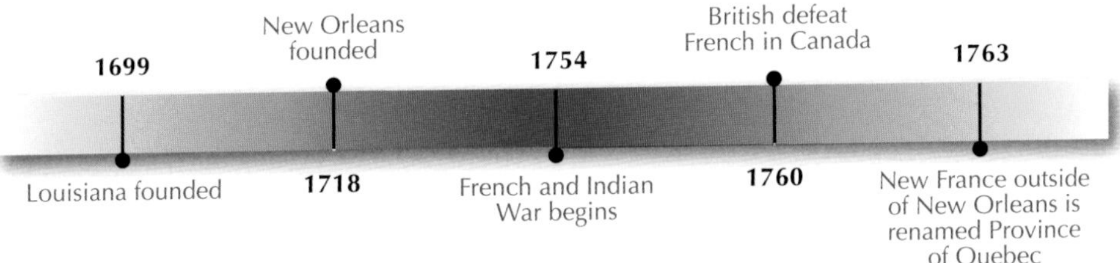
1699
Louisiana founded
New Orleans founded
1718
1754
French and Indian War begins
British defeat French in Canada
1760
1763
New France outside of New Orleans is renamed Province of Quebec

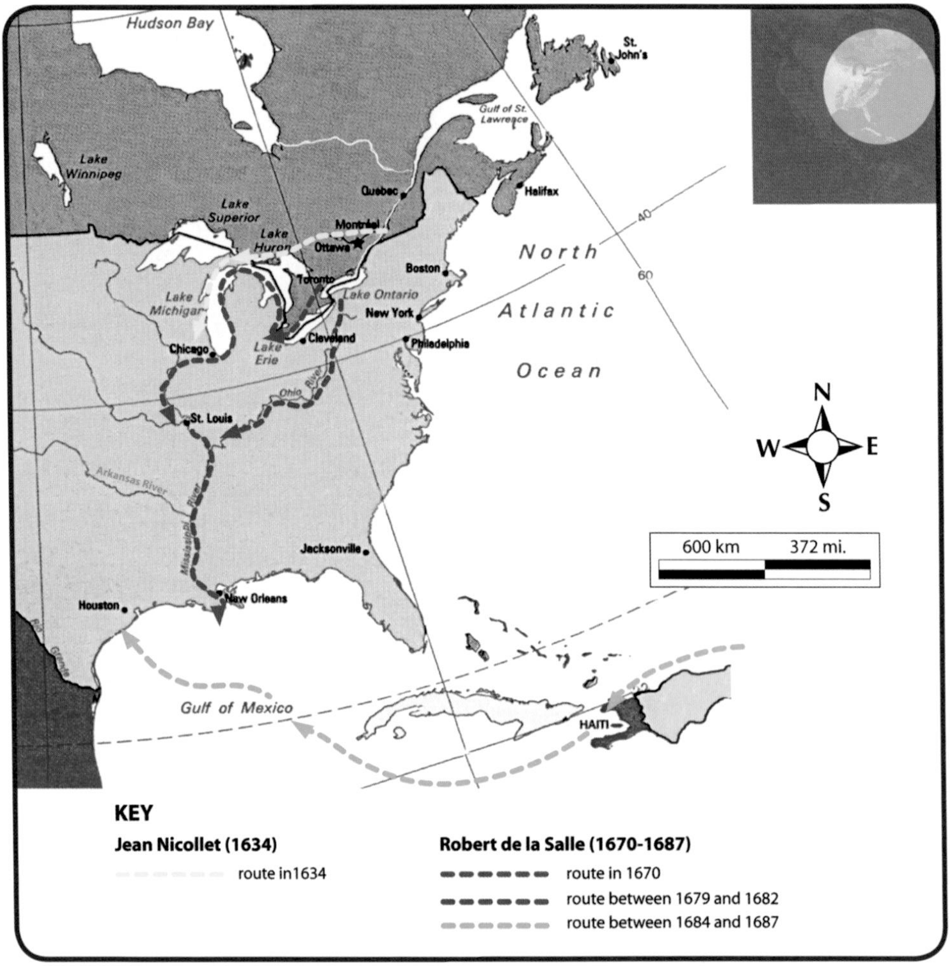

Chapter 2

Hudson Bay
St. John's
Gulf of St. Lawrence
Lake Winnipeg
Quebec
Halifax
Lake Superior
Lake Huron
Montréal
Ottawa
Boston
Toronto
Lake Ontario
North Atlantic Ocean
Lake Michigan
New York
Chicago
Lake Erie
Cleveland
Philadelphia
Ohio River
St. Louis
Arkansas River
Mississippi River
Jacksonville
Houston
New Orleans
Rio Grande
Gulf of Mexico
HAITI
N
W
E
S
600 km
372 mi.

KEY

Jean Nicollet (1634)

route in1634

Robert de la Salle (1670-1687)

route in 1670

route between 1679 and 1682

route between 1684 and 1687

The French explorers of North America were every bit as intrepid as their Spanish and Portuguese counterparts. Following the river system that supplied them with beaver, they ranged over thousands of miles from the Atlantic Ocean to the Gulf of Mexico. Joliet and Marquette made it down the Mississippi River as far as the Arkansas River.

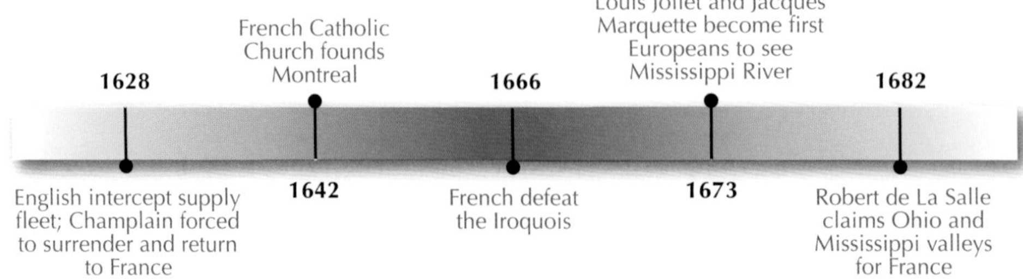

their trade routes. The English edged farther into the North American interior. Hostilities soon increased between the two superpowers.

Events in New France were often dictated by what was happening in Europe. The ruling powers there used their New World holdings like poker chips. At the end of the War of the Spanish Succession in 1713, France gave up some of its New France territories to the Spanish and British. Its territories of Acadia, Newfoundland, and Hudson's Bay went to England, but for many years this transfer was in name only.[16]

The interior of Canada from Quebec to the Great Lakes stayed in French control. The experienced French military and their Indian allies held firm. Farmland made inroads into the dense forests. Industries such as shipbuilding and ironworks grew, as did the population.

Another war in Europe caused renewed hostilities between the English and French in the New World. After the War of the Austrian Succession (1740–1748) in Europe, England was determined to continue the conflict with the French. The English were particularly interested in taking control of the Ohio Valley area in North America. This land was rich in game and resources, especially furs.

More importantly, the Ohio River fed into the Mississippi River. From that point, one could go anywhere. To the north, the Mississippi led to the Great Lakes, the St. Lawrence River, and the Atlantic Ocean. To the south, it led to the Atlantic via the Gulf of Mexico.

In 1753, English settlers became especially concerned about the French presence along the Ohio River on the western edges of the English colonies. George Washington, then a young officer in the Virginia militia, traveled to the French Fort LeBoeuf. He asked the French commander to abandon the fort. The commander refused. The following year, Washington was the leader of British troops who killed a

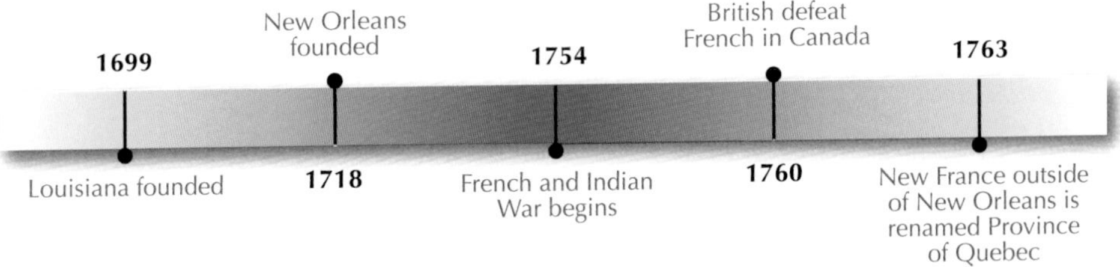
1699
Louisiana founded
New Orleans founded
1718
1754
French and Indian War begins
British defeat French in Canada
1760
1763
New France outside of New Orleans is renamed Province of Quebec

George Washington, general during the American Revolution and first president of the United States of America. Washington gained early military experience during the French and Indian War.

French soldier. This action sparked the French and Indian War.

The war began with English attacks on French forts in western Canada.[17] At first they did not succeed. The French and Indians were better fighters. But as the war wore on, the French made mistakes. In 1759 Quebec fell, then Montreal in 1760.[18]

The French and Indian War ended when the Treaty of Paris was signed in 1763. Under the terms of the treaty, Louisiana also slipped from France's fingers. It was traded to Spain in a series of complex negotiations.

And so the era of New France ended. The vast territories stretching from Hudson's Bay to the Gulf of Mexico had proved impossible to keep with so few colonists. The legacy of the French remained in the language, place names, and forms of government, but after 1763, New France—with the exception of some small islands—belonged to England.[19]

The Fur Trade

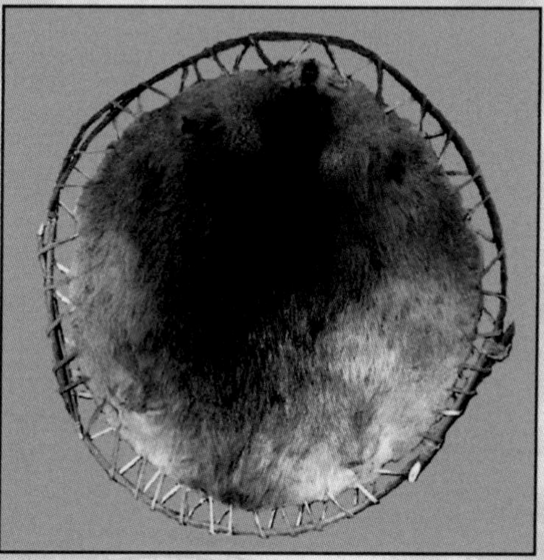
Beaver pelt

The fur trade was one of the most important moneymakers in the New World. There were many fur-bearing creatures in North America, but beaver fur, in particular, was prized for its fine quality. Beaver pelts were thick, strong, waterproof, and attractive. They were used to make hats. Beaver fur hats had become popular in the Middle Ages. They remained so until the mid-1800s.

Beavers are an ancient species. The prehistoric beaver was as big as a bear, with sharp cutting teeth a foot long. The giant beaver died out thousands of years ago. The beavers of the fur trade era were the same size as the beavers of today, about two feet long plus tail.

Beavers were once plentiful in Europe. They lived anywhere there was plenty of water. But because of the fur hat craze, they were hunted almost to extinction. When Europeans found beavers in North America, they thought they had hit the jackpot.

Beaver fur hats were not made from the actual fur of the beaver, like the coonskin cap made famous by Daniel Boone. In fact, the outer fur—the visible part—was usually removed to get at the shorter inner coat. This inner coat was warm, soft, and easy to shape. For beavers, having two coats worked the same way layered clothing works for us. That extra inner layer helped the beaver stay warm and dry in cold and wet conditions.

This inner layer could be treated with a variety of chemicals that would turn it into felt. Felt kept some of the same qualities of the beaver fur. It was warm and sturdy. Felt was easy to cut and form. It could be made into hats of many different shapes and sizes.

What did Europeans trade for a beaver pelt? Trade goods varied, depending on the Indians they were trading with and the quality of the pelt. A 1795 trading guide suggested "two silver crosses, [or] eight knives, [or] two hatchet heads."[20] One large beaver pelt could make as many as eighteen hats. By some estimates, beaver pelts sold in Europe for twenty times what they cost in the New World.[21]

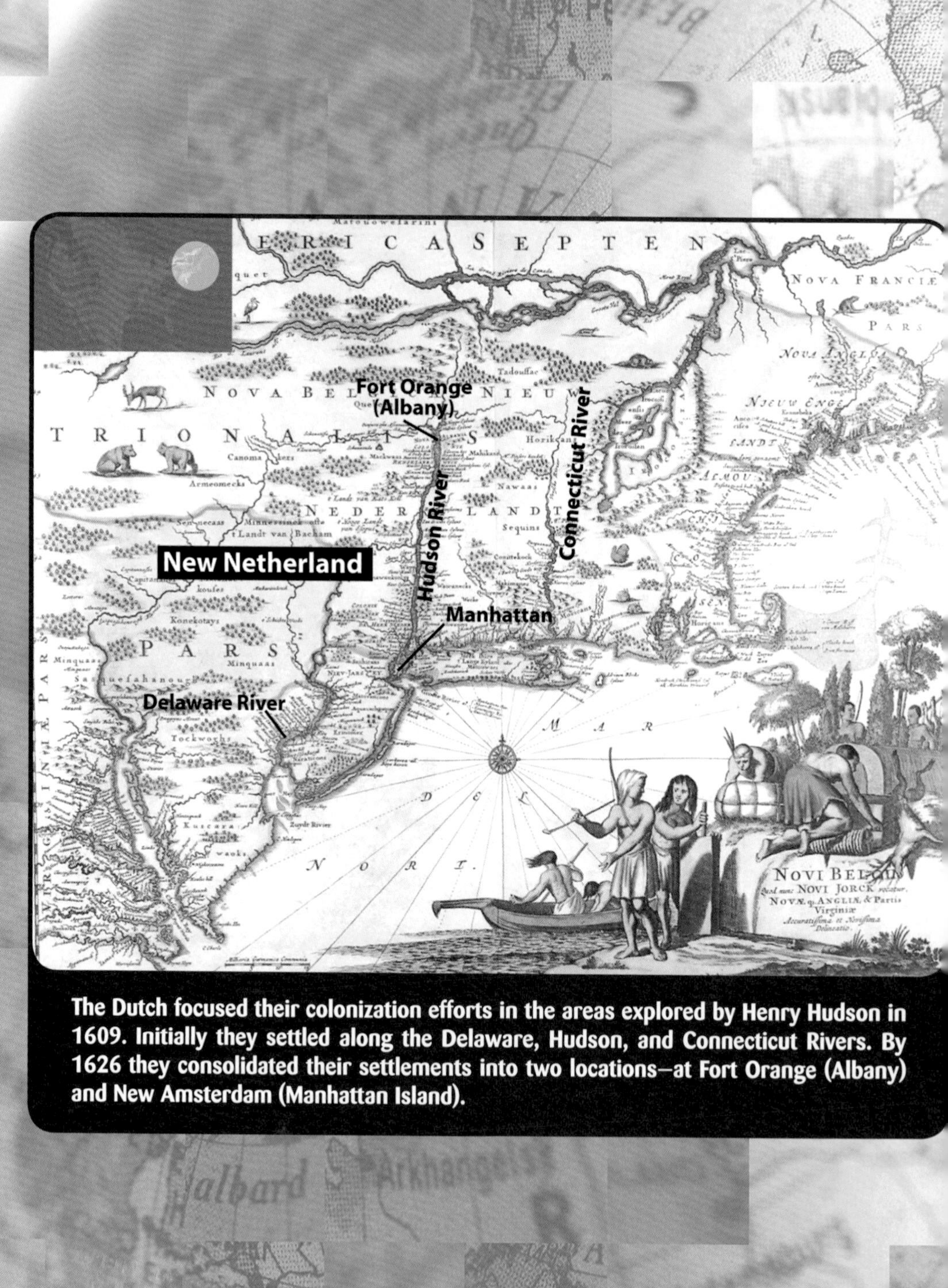

The Dutch focused their colonization efforts in the areas explored by Henry Hudson in 1609. Initially they settled along the Delaware, Hudson, and Connecticut Rivers. By 1626 they consolidated their settlements into two locations—at Fort Orange (Albany) and New Amsterdam (Manhattan Island).

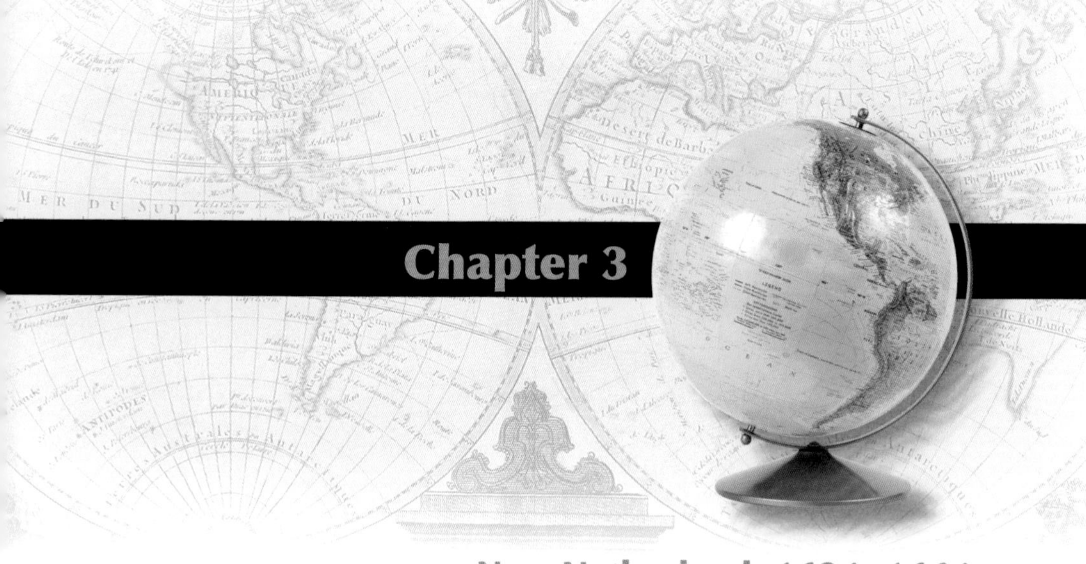

Chapter 3

New Netherland, 1624–1664

Situated on the coast of the North Sea in northern Europe, the Netherlands has a grand history as a trading and seafaring power. During the age of exploration of the New World, the country's momentum grew as one of the major powers of Europe. The great exploring empires of Spain and Portugal were past their peak, but England and the Netherlands were on the rise.

The Dutch were determined not to be left behind in the race for the New World. They were in the hunt to find a western route to China. The great Dutch trading concern, the East India Company, hired the famous English sea captain Henry Hudson in 1609 to sail for them. Hudson, too, was infected with China fever. It was his dream to find a shorter sea route to the riches of the East. The Dutch provided Hudson with a crew and ship, the *Half Moon*. His orders were to find an eastern route over Russia, which he promptly ignored. He sailed west.[1]

In August Hudson became the first European to enter Delaware Bay. He proceeded north into present-day New York Harbor, where he met with some of the Indians. He surveyed the area as a possible trade center. Hudson sailed up the river that now bears his name until he realized it would not take him to China. Upon his return to the Netherlands, his glowing reports sent the businesslike Dutch into a frenzy. They were especially excited to hear of a fresh source of beaver pelts. The Dutch claimed the lands Hudson explored as their own. They rubbed their hands in glee over the business opportunities it offered.[2]

Henry Hudson sailed on the *Half Moon* with sixteen crewmen. They explored the North American coast in 1609 on behalf of the Netherlands, seeking a western trade route to Asia.

Henry Hudson had no particular interest in business. He was determined to find a route to China. So he and the Dutch parted ways. Hudson found other backers for his quest, and the Dutch had their toehold in the New World.[3] They called it New Netherland. The actual administration of the new colony was in the hands of the West India Company. Its headquarters were in the Netherlands.

In 1624 a shipload of Dutch settlers landed in what is now New York Harbor. They built scattered dwellings along the Delaware, Hudson, and Connecticut Rivers. A handful of settlers here, another handful there, were expected to defend hundreds of miles of territory. It was a bad idea. These lands were already occupied, of course. A variety of Native American tribes lived there, including the Mohawks, Mohicans, Lenapes, and others. Between problems with the natives and conflicts with colony leadership, the Dutch were off to a shaky start.[4]

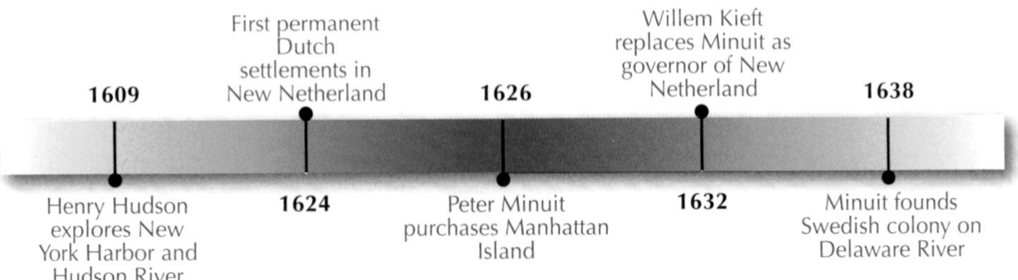
1609
Henry Hudson explores New York Harbor and Hudson River
1624
First permanent Dutch settlements in New Netherland
1626
Peter Minuit purchases Manhattan Island
1632
Willem Kieft replaces Minuit as governor of New Netherland
1638
Minuit founds Swedish colony on Delaware River

Enter one Peter Minuit. Minuit took over the operation of the Dutch colony in 1626. One of his first acts was to bring the colonists to a central location. But where? Ideally the location should be good for trade as well as transportation and survival. Minuit chose the southern tip of Manhattan Island. Then he made his famous purchase of the island for the now legendary twenty-four dollars' worth of trade goods.[5]

The settlement was called New Amsterdam. Minuit maintained a small outpost at Fort Orange, today's Albany, because it was closer to the Indians with whom they were trading. New Amsterdam was a hodgepodge of people from many different backgrounds. Tradesmen and soldiers, thieves and pirates populated the ragtag town. Individual homes and businesses gradually sprang up.[6]

Minuit spent several years running the colony. In 1632 he got into trouble with his bosses back in the Netherlands. They fired him. Minuit wasted no time contacting friends who knew of another opportunity for him in the New World.[7]*

New Netherland struggled along, barely turning a profit on beaver pelts. There were plenty of pelts—that wasn't the problem. The West India Company had invested a great deal of money in ships and supplies for New Netherland. It was going to take a lot of pelts to earn that money back, much less make a profit.[8]

The colony was set up as a trading monopoly. This meant that any profits made on pelts and other trade goods went to the West India Company. The colonists couldn't trade on their own. They were little

*See Chapter 4.

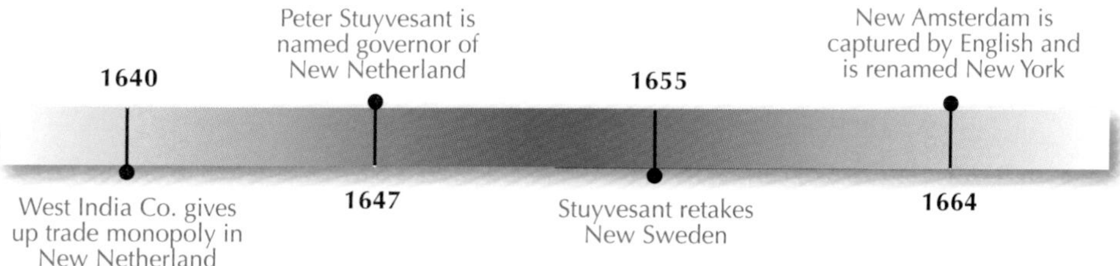
1640
West India Co. gives up trade monopoly in New Netherland
Peter Stuyvesant is named governor of New Netherland
1647
1655
Stuyvesant retakes New Sweden
New Amsterdam is captured by English and is renamed New York
1664

Peter Minuit (center) traded trinkets worth approximately $24 for Manhattan Island. Minuit later bought Staten Island for tools, woven cloth called duffel, and wampum.

more than peasants working for the big corporation, barely making ends meet. In addition, they faced stiff trade competition from the French and the English. Both groups were experienced traders, often offering better prices to the natives for their pelts. The English caused further friction by settling in nearby Connecticut in territory that New Netherland claimed as its own.

With the colony on the brink of collapse, the West India Company abandoned its trade monopoly. In 1640 they turned the colony into a

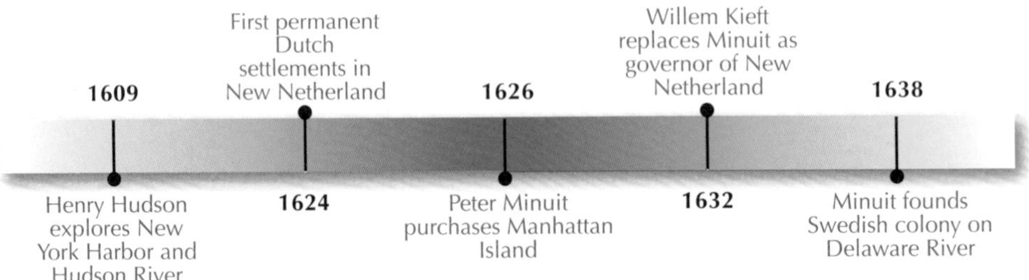
1609
Henry Hudson explores New York Harbor and Hudson River
1624
First permanent Dutch settlements in New Netherland
1626
Peter Minuit purchases Manhattan Island
1632
Willem Kieft replaces Minuit as governor of New Netherland
1638
Minuit founds Swedish colony on Delaware River

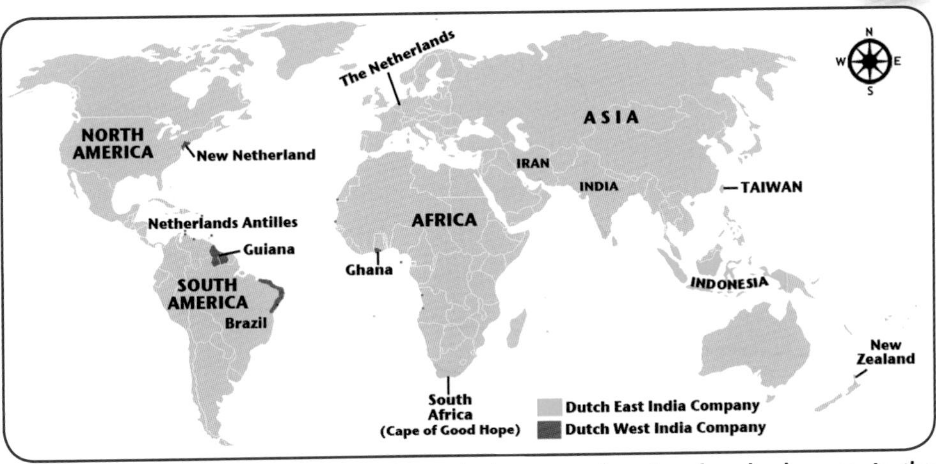

The Dutch were leaders in worldwide trade for more than two hundred years. In the seventeenth century, the Dutch had colonies and trading posts all over the world, including New Netherland and Netherlands Antilles.

free market. Colonists could now work and trade for themselves as well as for the West India Company. Almost overnight, New Netherland was transformed from a miserable collection of colonists barely scraping by to a grand land of opportunity.[9]

A free market was a perfect environment for the hardworking Dutch. Unlike the other major European empires, the Dutch didn't care about royal family connections or noble titles. They believed anyone could get ahead in life with the right amount of effort and ability. New Amsterdam quickly prospered. By opening up their monopoly on the fur trade, the West India Company could now more easily attract permanent settlers to New Netherland.[10]

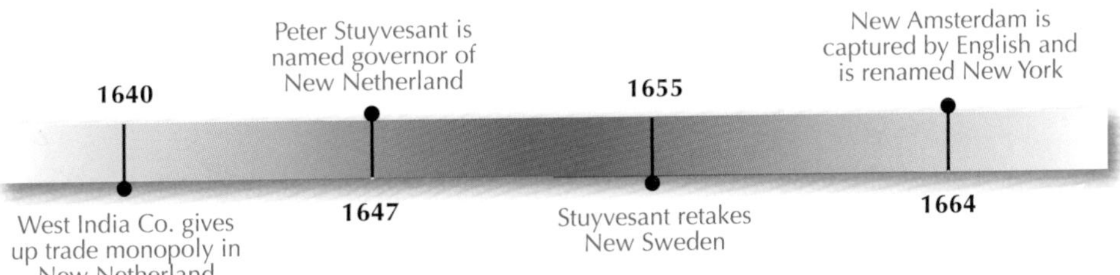

The colonists profited at the expense of the company. Much of the money that used to flow into company accounts now stayed in the pockets of the colonists. The company pressured the new director of the colony, Willem Kieft, for more profits. In order to accomplish this, Kieft put some new policies into place that were very unpopular with the colonists. He restricted the type of wampum that could be used for trade. He proposed that the Indians pay a tax to support the Dutch forts in their territory. The colonists knew these two decisions would

Willem Kieft (in red) plots with Dutch colleagues against the Indians. Kieft ran the New Netherland colony from 1638 to 1647.

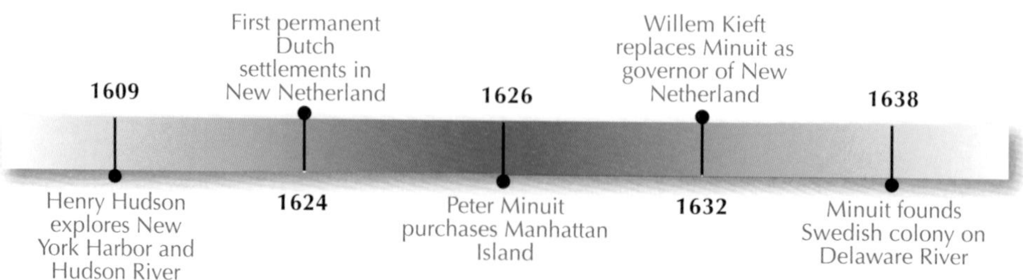

1609
Henry Hudson explores New York Harbor and Hudson River
1624
First permanent Dutch settlements in New Netherland
1626
Peter Minuit purchases Manhattan Island
1632
Willem Kieft replaces Minuit as governor of New Netherland
1638
Minuit founds Swedish colony on Delaware River

be unpopular with the local tribes. They feared a decline in their trading business, or worse. They also resented Kieft's refusal to include them in the colony's decision-making process.[11]

Relations soon deteriorated between the Dutch and the Indians. The colonists' worst fears were realized. In 1643 Kieft's policies led to a period of devastating hostilities between the natives and the Dutch. Much of the hard work of the past decades was lost as battles raged within the colony. The colonists were forced to abandon their homes and withdraw into the safety of the forts in New Amsterdam and Fort Orange. They soon demanded a change in colony leadership. In 1647 the West India Company replaced Kieft with Peter Stuyvesant.[12]

Peter Stuyvesant replaced Willem Kieft in 1647. A former military man, he served as governor of New Netherland until its takeover by the British in 1664. It was during his tenure that the wall of Wall Street fame was built.

Stuyvesant was a tough man. He was a veteran of the Dutch West India operations in the Caribbean. While there, he had lost one of his lower legs during a battle for a Spanish fort. It had been replaced with a wooden peg.

Stuyvesant was aware of the colony's problems. Their Indian trading partners were unhappy. The English colonists edged closer to Dutch territory

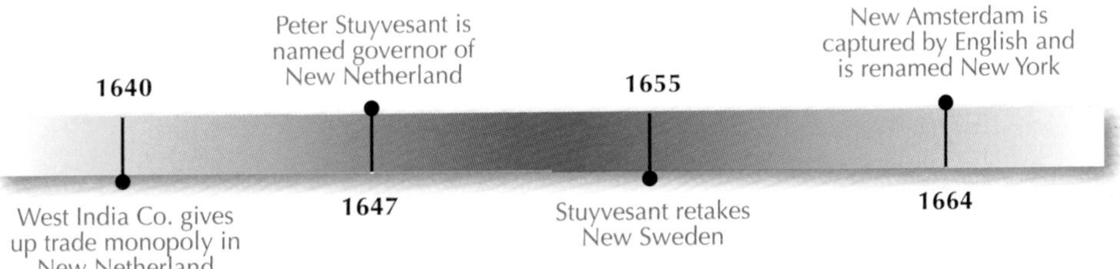
1640
West India Co. gives up trade monopoly in New Netherland
Peter Stuyvesant is named governor of New Netherland
1647
1655
Stuyvesant retakes New Sweden
New Amsterdam is captured by English and is renamed New York
1664

to the north. The Swedes occupied Dutch lands to the south. Even his own colonists were upset. They had not liked Kieft and felt Stuyvesant was no improvement. They wanted more say in how the colony was run. While the colonists argued for more representation in the governance of New Amsterdam, Stuyvesant barely clung to his job. On the verge of being fired, his job was saved when war broke out between the Dutch and the English in 1652. As an experienced military man, Stuyvesant kept his position.[13]

The Dutch and English made peace in 1654. Able to relax about a possible English invasion, Stuyvesant had the time and manpower to address the Swedish situation. In 1655 he led a force of ships and soldiers to Delaware Bay and took back the area for the Dutch.[14]

Once again events in Europe foreshadowed change for the New World colonies. George Downing, England's ambassador to the Netherlands, hated the Dutch. He used his influence with England's King Charles II to drive the Dutch out of North America.[15]

English raiders attacked Dutch holdings in the Cape Verde Islands and Africa's Guinea Coast at the end of 1663. In March the following year, under Downing's influence, Charles granted his brother James, Duke of York, much of the land from Maine to Delaware. The grant included New Netherland. At the end of May, Charles sent a squadron of English ships to America, all the while assuring the Dutch there was no evil intent. This was a bald-faced lie.[16]

The English squadron anchored off Manhattan and demanded that the Dutch surrender. Military man that he was, Stuyvesant wanted to resist. But the citizens of New Amsterdam did not want to see their homes and businesses destroyed or lives lost. The citizens prevailed. Stuyvesant reluctantly negotiated a surrender with the English.[17]

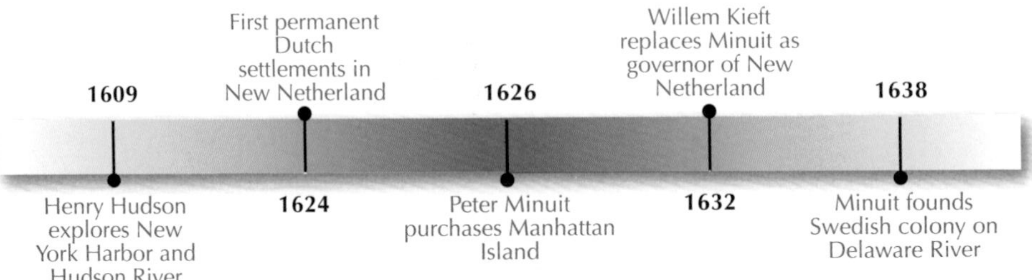
1609
Henry Hudson explores New York Harbor and Hudson River
1624
First permanent Dutch settlements in New Netherland
1626
Peter Minuit purchases Manhattan Island
1632
Willem Kieft replaces Minuit as governor of New Netherland
1638
Minuit founds Swedish colony on Delaware River

i: HEERE GRACHT.
j: PRINCE GRACHT.
k: BEGIJN GRACHT.
l: HOOGH STRAET.
m: PAEREL STRAET.
n: TUYN STRAET.
o: HEERE DWARS STRAET.
p: SLYCK STEEG.
q: BRUGH STRAET.
r: STADT HUYS LAAN.
s: HET MARCKVELT STEEGIE.
t: HET BEVER PAD.
u: BROUWER STRAET.

Noort Rivier

Anchorage

DE HEERE STRAET

FORT AMSTERDAM

HET MARCKVELT

PRINCE STRAET

SMEE STRAET

HET CINGEL

THE WALL

Schreijer's Hoek

the *City* of *New Amsterdam*
on the *Island* of *Manhattan*
in the *Colony* of *New Netherland*. Anno 1660

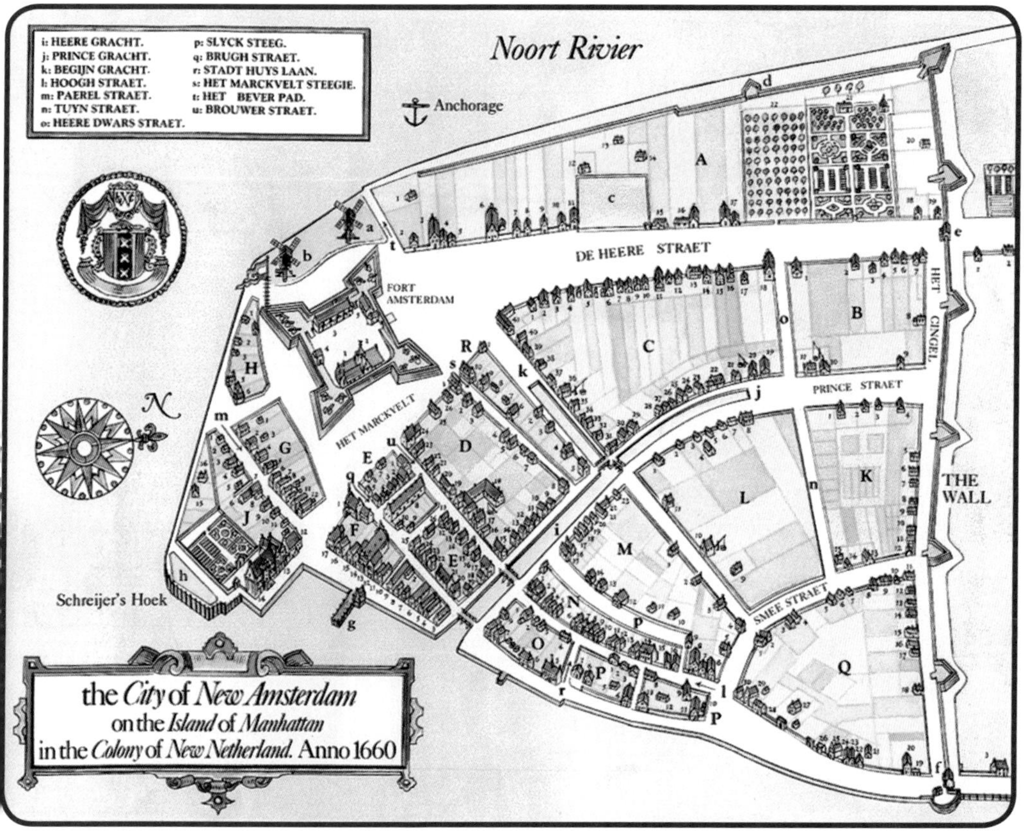

Fort Amsterdam and "The Wall" are clearly visible in this map of New Amsterdam. Note that North is to the right, rather than at the top. The Noort Rivier is the Hudson River.

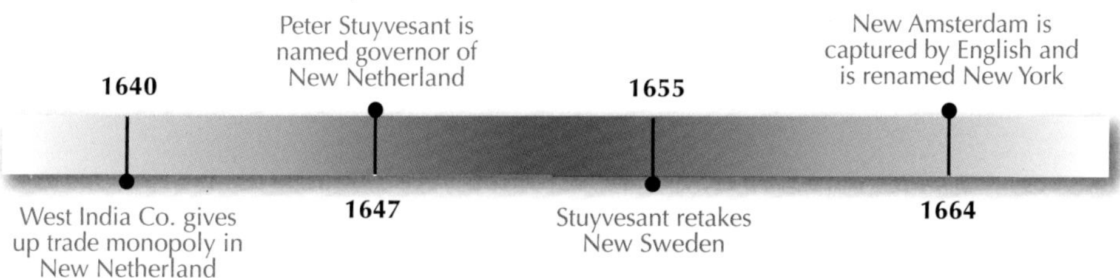
1640
West India Co. gives up trade monopoly in New Netherland
Peter Stuyvesant is named governor of New Netherland
1647
1655
Stuyvesant retakes New Sweden
New Amsterdam is captured by English and is renamed New York
1664

King Charles II (left) ruled England from 1649 to 1660. Upon his death, his brother James, Duke of York (right), became king. The two brothers ruled England during the early colonial periods in America.

The terms of the surrender were friendly. The English allowed the Dutch to keep many of their existing customs. They were free to travel and to continue trading. They kept their local governmental structures. Religious and personal freedoms continued as before. However, there was one change. New Amsterdam was quickly renamed New York, after the Duke of York. No one realized at the time that the little town would eventually become one of the greatest cities in the world.[18]

For Your Information

The Lenapes

Peter Minuit bought Manhattan Island from the Lenape Indians (also known as the Delaware Indians). When the Europeans arrived in North America, there were as many as 25,000 Lenapes already there. They lived in settlements scattered from the Delaware River north to the Hudson River. Their coastal lands were the source of the shells used to make wampum.[19]

Lenape (leh-NAH-pay) means "common people." The Lenapes lived simply. They grew corn, squash, and beans. The men hunted and fished. They made tools from stone, antlers, and wood. Their homes were designed to be moved easily. As the weather changed and their food supplies shifted, so did the Lenapes.[20]

Europeans reported the Lenapes as well-formed, healthy people. They wore deerskin clothing in cold weather. In warm weather they wore very little. The women wore their hair long, but the younger men removed most of theirs. They sometimes painted their faces red or yellow on special occasions or when going to war. The Lenape wore jewelry made of shells and stones. They tattooed their skin.[21]

Each of the Lenape villages, or clans, had a different name. Some were named for animals, like "turtle" or "wolf." Hackensack, New Jersey; Rockaway, New York; and Manhattan Island are among the present-day cities that take their names from Lenape clans.[22]

Lenape village

The arrival of the Europeans changed the Lenape lifestyle. The Lenapes spent less time hunting for food so they could hunt beaver. At first, they carried on a busy trade with the white settlers.[23] They enjoyed the tools and trinkets they received. Eventually the trade system fell apart. The beaver disappeared from Lenape lands due to over-hunting. Other tribes took over their lands to get the valuable wampum shells. The Lenape also had disagreements with the Europeans over land.

The Lenape Indians fought many battles with white settlers. They maintained a fierce fighting force. But there were too many whites. The Lenapes were driven out of their homelands. They were promised new homes and new lands, but the promises never lasted long. By the early 1900s, less than 2,000 Lenapes were left. Most lived in Oklahoma, while others lived in Wisconsin, Kansas, and Canada.[24]

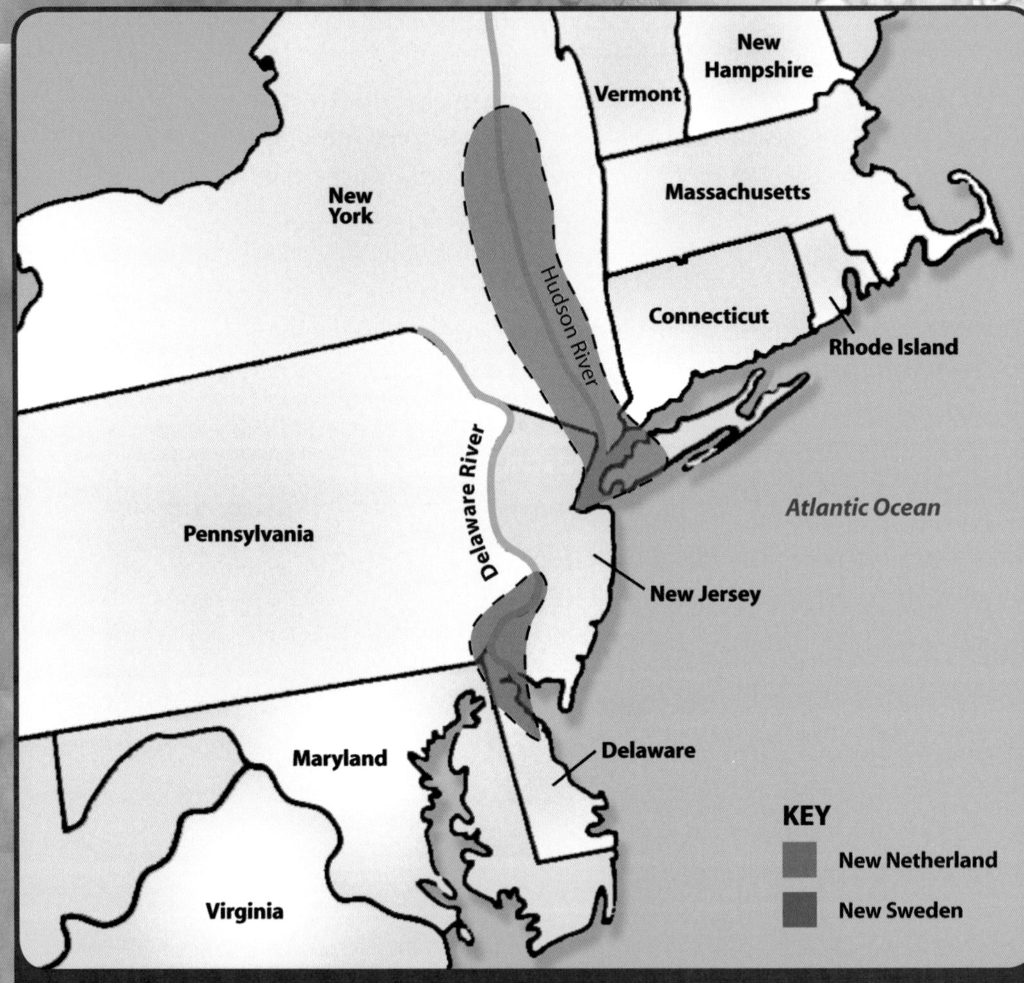

Peter Minuit targeted the Delaware River as a prime location for the New Sweden colony. Technically this area was claimed by New Netherland. But Minuit knew the Dutch were concentrated much farther north, in New Amsterdam and beyond. They had done little with the lands to the south. The map shows where these early colonies were in relation to present-day states.

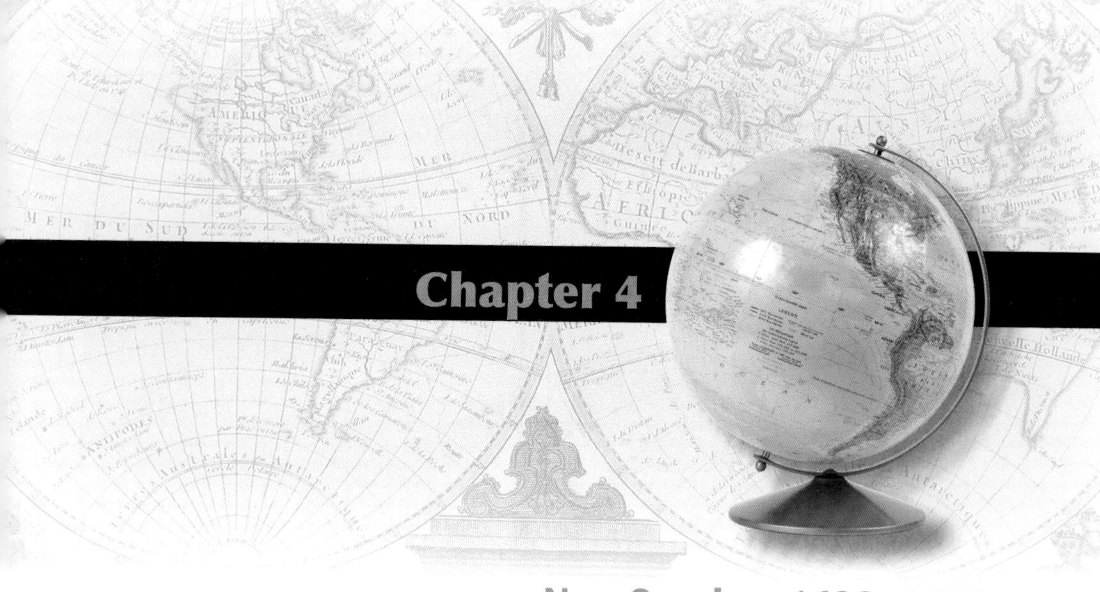

Chapter 4

New Sweden, 1638–1655

In the early 1600s Sweden was the strongest military power in Northern Europe. Its political control extended over Finland, parts of Norway, and other countries bordering the Baltic Sea. Coming off major military victories, Sweden was in a position to join the other major European powers in staking a claim in the New World.

Count Axel Oxenstierna, chancellor to Queen Christina, hoped the New World could provide a new market for Sweden's vast copper resources. He approached a Dutchman, Samuel Blommaert, who had experience in the New World.[1]

Blommaert had once worked for the Dutch West India Company. While there, he became a friend of Peter Minuit. Both Blommaert and Minuit agreed that the New World had great potential. Rather than simply seeking new markets, the two men suggested that Sweden found a colony in North America. They knew an ideal leader—Minuit himself.

Sweden kept its plan for a new colony secret. The last thing they wanted was for the Dutch to find out they were planning to start a colony in the Delaware River Valley. This area was part of the land that the Dutch had claimed for New Netherland.[2]

Under Minuit's command, two ships arrived at Delaware Bay in March 1638. The Swedes bought some land from the local Indians, the Lenapes. The colonists began construction of Fort Christina, named in honor of their queen. The fort was built at what is now Wilmington, Delaware.[3]

Count Axel Oxenstierna (left) served as chancellor, or adviser, to King Gustavus Adolphus of Sweden. Upon Gustavus' death in 1632, the only heir to the throne was six-year-old Christina (right). Oxenstierna helped govern Sweden until Queen Christina turned eighteen. He continued to advise her throughout her reign.

At this point, the Swedes made perhaps their most important contribution to North American culture. They were the first to build log cabins.[4] Log cabins are made of long logs, sometimes cut lengthwise, stacked on top of each other to form the walls. The log cabin became the definitive dwelling for the westward expansion that was to come.

It didn't take long for the Dutch to find out what the Swedes were up to. Willem Kieft, governor of New Netherland, had too many other

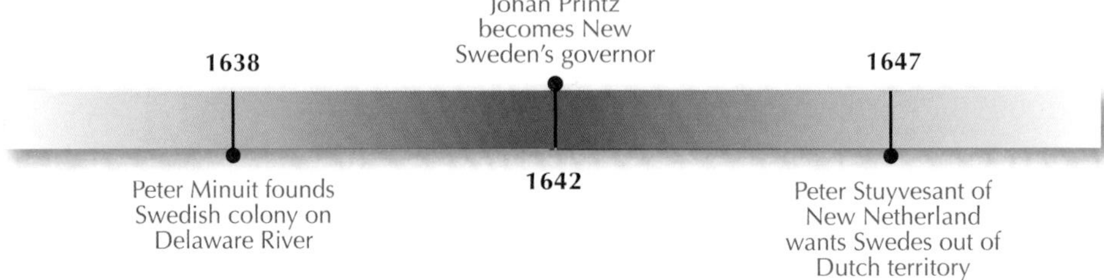
Johan Printz becomes New Sweden's governor
1638
1647
1642
Peter Minuit founds Swedish colony on Delaware River
Peter Stuyvesant of New Netherland wants Swedes out of Dutch territory

Wilmington, Delaware, located on the Christina River. Fort Christina Park in downtown Wilmington marks the former site of Fort Christina.

issues to concern him. There wasn't much he could do but complain. The wily Minuit had already outbid the Dutch for pelts. His plan was to get the Swedish colony off to a good start and let the diplomats in Europe work out the territory issues.[5]

Confident his plan was working, Minuit loaded his first cargo of pelts. He decided to stop in the Caribbean to trade for some tobacco before returning to Sweden. He was killed when a hurricane swept through the area. Cut down in his prime, Minuit was nonetheless proved right about the North American location. Soon the pelts and tobacco far outstripped any profits Sweden would have made on copper exports.[6]

1651
Dutch build Fort Casimir on Delaware River
Swedes under new governor Johan Rising take Dutch Fort Casimir (now Fort Trinity)
1654
1655
Stuyvesant captures Fort Trinity from the Swedes

At first, the colony prospered. More Swedish ships arrived with supplies and colonists. The Swedes were definitely taking business away from the Dutch. The Dutch were not happy about it, but the two countries were at peace. Sweden was the more powerful of the two at that time. The Dutch feared if they took action against the Swedes, it might cause an international incident.[7]

The Swedes bought more land from their Indian neighbors. The new lands extended the colony north to present-day Trenton, New Jersey. More colonists and supplies arrived in 1641, including some settlers from Finland.[8]

A new governor, Johan Printz, was named the following year. Printz and the Dutch governor had a gentlemen's agreement that the Dutch would not settle on the west side of the Delaware. Indeed, the two colonies worked together to keep the English from advancing up the Delaware. This arrangement worked for both colonies until the Dutch realized it was hurting their pelt trade.

Johan Printz, governor of New Sweden. Printz was chosen for his military and administrative experience. His three-year commitment to the job stretched into ten—he arrived in 1643 and stayed until 1653.

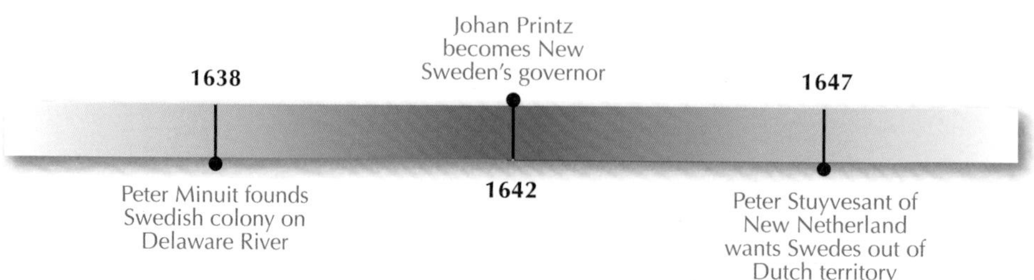
Johan Printz becomes New Sweden's governor
1638
1647
Peter Minuit founds Swedish colony on Delaware River
1642
Peter Stuyvesant of New Netherland wants Swedes out of Dutch territory

Gradually the Dutch began settling on the west side of the Delaware. Printz protested but was powerless. He had neither the supplies nor the manpower to take action. Nevertheless, the Swedes and the Dutch colonists to the north tolerated each other until 1647 and the arrival of Peter Stuyvesant. Stuyvesant wanted the Swedes out of Dutch territory, but he was under strict orders not to provoke an incident that might set off a war with one of Europe's greatest military powers.

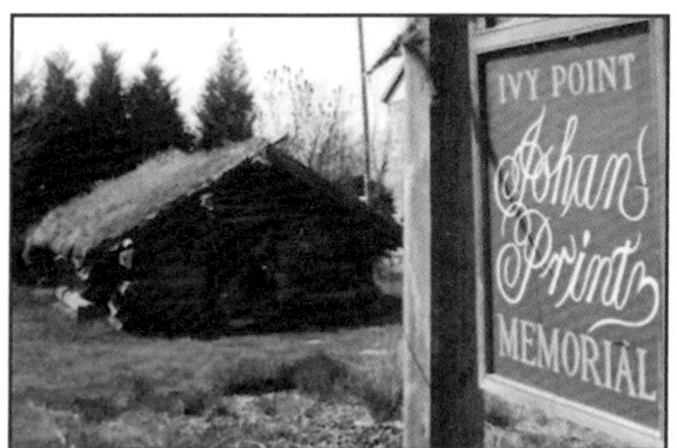
IVY POINT
Johan Printz
MEMORIAL

The Swedes were the first in America to build log cabins like this replica in Salem, New Jersey. Governor Printz, his wife, and five daughters arrived at Fort Christina in 1643. Their principal residence was on Tinicum Island in the Delaware River near Philadelphia.

Stuyvesant devised a plan to get rid of the Swedes. He had observed that Sweden was not supporting its colony. Supply ships rarely arrived from the homeland.[9] He planned to outposition the Swedes and run them out of the pelt trade. By the time help arrived, if it ever did, the Dutch would be back in charge of the area.

Stuyvesant encouraged Dutch colonists to settle in Swedish territory. In addition, he built a fort on the east bank of the Schuylkill River to better trade with the Indians. Printz did not have enough soldiers to do anything about this, and Stuyvesant knew it.

Banking on this knowledge, Stuyvesant took a bold step in 1651. The Swedes had forts on the east bank of the Delaware, but the west bank was unoccupied. Gathering a force of over one hundred men,

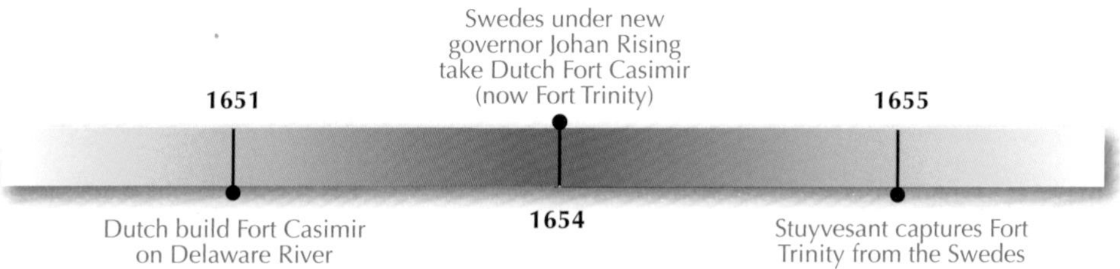
1651
Dutch build Fort Casimir on Delaware River
1654
Swedes under new governor Johan Rising take Dutch Fort Casimir (now Fort Trinity)
1655
Stuyvesant captures Fort Trinity from the Swedes

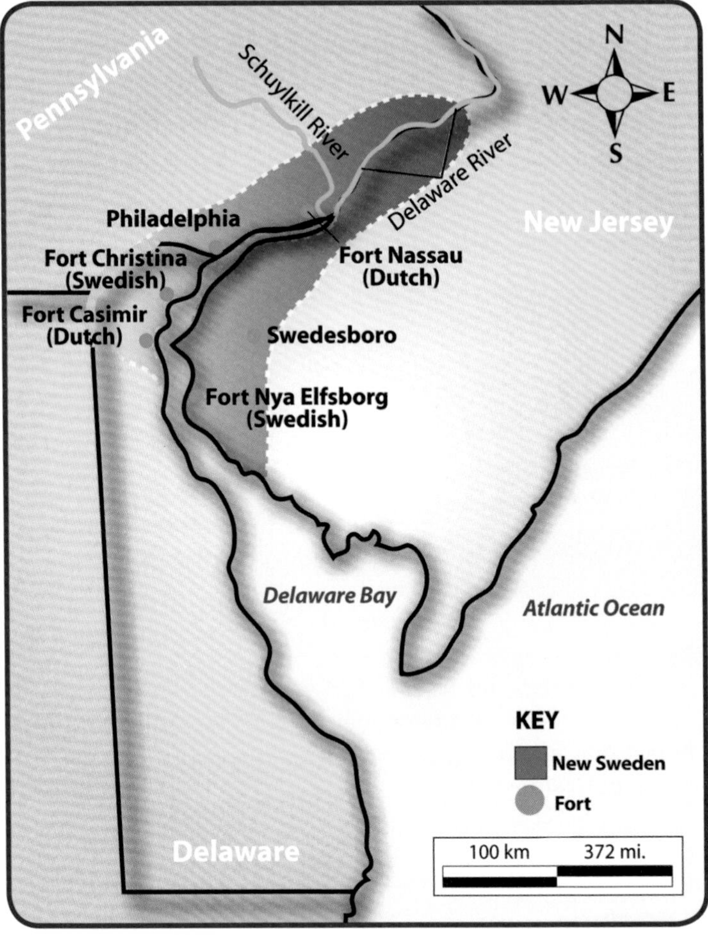

The Swedes and the Dutch built a checkerboard of forts along the Delaware. Each vied for the best positions for trade and defense. Peter Stuyvesant's construction of Fort Casimir proved to be the best location until the Dutch surrendered it to the Swedes in 1655. It was back in Dutch hands only a few months later.

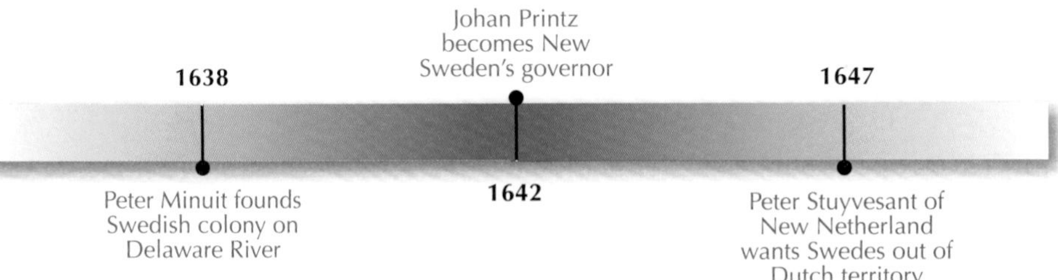

Stuyvesant marched south from the Dutch Fort Nassau (near Gloucester, New Jersey) and met with a fleet of Dutch ships at Delaware Bay. Together this impressive force moved up the river to a place on the west bank carefully selected by Stuyvesant. They began building Fort Casimir.[10]

The Swedes protested, as they felt they had purchased this land from the Indians that long-ago day in 1638. In the end, they had no choice but to sit and watch.

By that point New Sweden was struggling. It was not yet able to grow enough food. No ships had arrived from home since 1648. With the absence of fresh supplies, the colonists relied heavily on trade with the English to the south and would have starved without it.[11]

To make matters worse, the colonists were unhappy with Printz. They resented his heavy-handed control of the colony. Printz himself was unhappy and constantly asked his superiors to replace him.[12]

In Sweden, support for the new colony waned. Sweden had been at war with Denmark. Supporting the war was more important to Queen Christina than the needs of the colony. For a time it looked as if the colony would die of neglect.[13]

Then the Swedish economy experienced a decline. Famine spread through the land. Suddenly, New Sweden looked very attractive to struggling Swedes. Chancellor Oxenstierna, still working for the queen, named a new colonial governor, Johan Rising. Rising and 350 settlers sailed for the colony in 1654. It was an unlucky journey. An epidemic broke out on board, killing more than 100. There was some good news when they landed. The nearby Dutch fort across the river, Fort Casimir, was practically abandoned. Most of its soldiers had been recalled to defend New Netherland from the British.[14]

Swedes under new governor Johan Rising take Dutch Fort Casimir (now Fort Trinity)
1651
1655
Dutch build Fort Casimir on Delaware River
1654
Stuyvesant captures Fort Trinity from the Swedes

Rising marched his men to Fort Casimir and easily took it. He renamed it Fort Trefaldighet (Trinity). Sailing on to Fort Christina, Rising settled in and took charge. The new influx of Swedish colonists, though reduced in number by the epidemic, outnumbered the Dutch in the area. Both groups agreed to live peaceably.[15]

In spite of new leadership, times were difficult. Under Rising, the colony's economy improved somewhat. But the Indians feared trading with the Swedes because of the epidemic. The Swedes were forced to travel farther and pay more for pelts.

A supply ship finally sailed from Sweden, but it stopped in New Amsterdam on the way to Fort Trinity. Stuyvesant confiscated it in retaliation for Rising taking Fort Casimir. The Swedes got by that winter as best they could and hoped for a better year to follow.[16]

Meanwhile the Dutch made peace with the English, leaving Stuyvesant free to pursue his revenge against the Swedes. Stuyvesant led a flotilla of seven ships into Delaware Bay in 1655 and captured Fort Trinity. The Dutch moved upriver to Fort Christina and surrounded it. Rising refused to give up. The Dutch burned the Swedish settlements nearby, although no deaths were recorded. Eventually Rising realized he didn't have enough men or supplies to resist the Dutch. On September 15, 1655, Rising surrendered. This was the end of New Sweden.[17]

For Your Information

Peter Minuit

Peter Minuit was born around 1580 in the German city of Wesel, near the border with the Netherlands. As an adult he married and worked as a diamond cutter in the Netherlands. He wasn't happy in his work. He heard about the Dutch West India Company's venture to the New World. In 1624 he volunteered to go.

Minuit made an impression on his fellow colonists. He was a hard worker and had many good ideas. In 1626 he was named governor of New Netherland. As the colony grew, Minuit made a few enemies among the colonists. He and his bosses disagreed about how best to run the colony. In 1632, they fired him.

Minuit was unfazed. He knew if he had a chance to run a colony his way, it would succeed. He heard about another opportunity in the New World. Sweden wanted to do business there. They were looking for someone to lead the venture. Minuit's experience with New Netherland made him the perfect man for the job. In 1638 he returned to the New World. He landed in present-day Delaware and founded New Sweden.

New Sweden's colonists benefited from Minuit's experience. They built a fort, purchased land, and began trading with the Indians right away. Minuit felt things were going well. He decided to return to Sweden to make a report. On the way, he stopped at an island in the Caribbean to trade for some tobacco. He ran into an old friend one evening and joined him aboard the friend's ship. A hurricane blew in, and the friend's ship disappeared. Ironically, Minuit's ship was unharmed during the storm.

Monuments to Peter Minuit are few. In New York City, a plaza and a public school are named for him. There is a marker bearing his name at the site where he bought Manhattan. Perhaps the greatest monument to Minuit is Manhattan Island itself. Minuit thought it had potential to be the center of commerce in the New World. He was right.[18]

Twentieth-century Manhattan

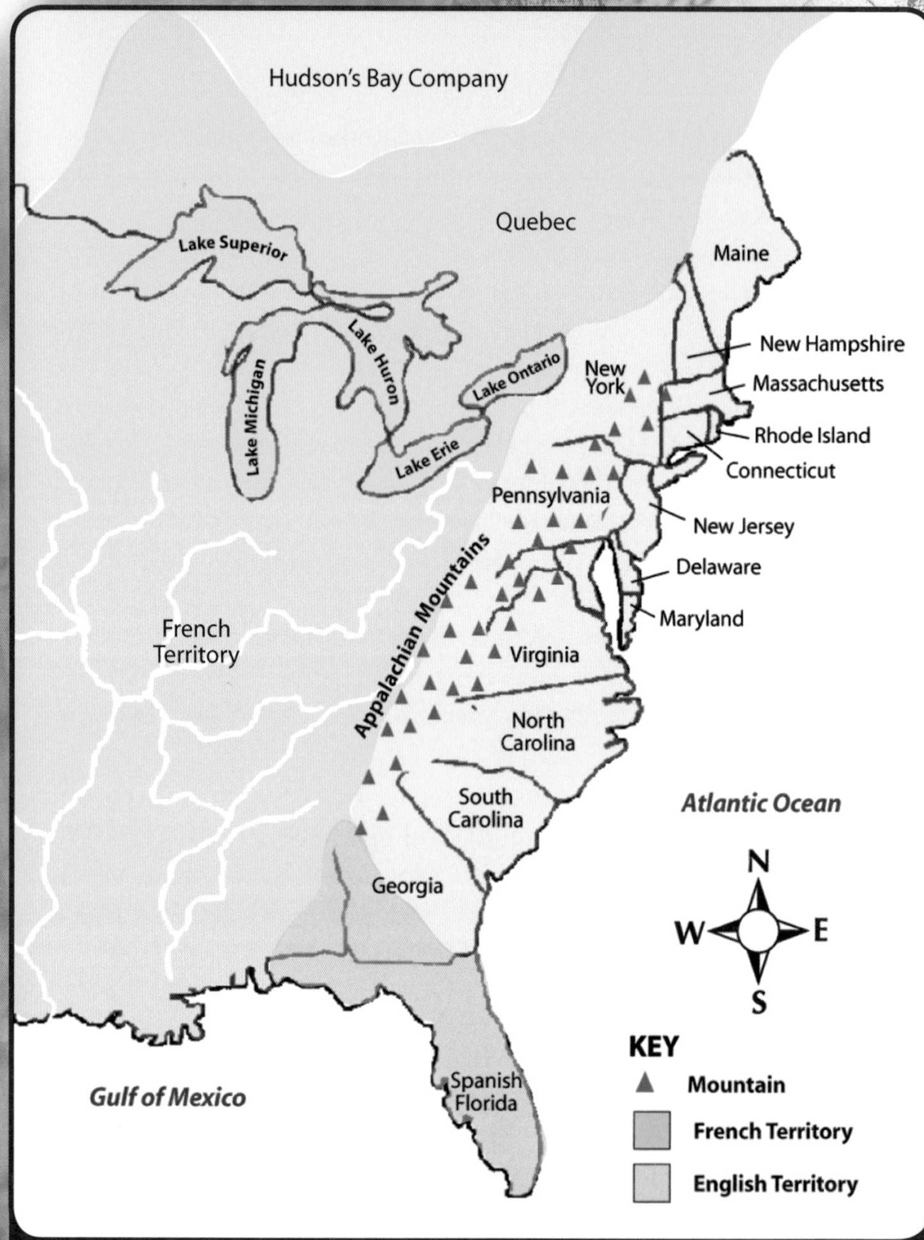

The American Revolution dramatically changed British holdings in North America. British influence, once widespread up and down the Atlantic coast, now halted abruptly at Maine's border with Canada. If it wished to expand into the continent, Britain was forced to look to the north and west.

Chapter 5

Canada, 1763–1867

When the British took over New France, they renamed it the Province of Quebec.[1] It got off to a rocky start as a British colony. The French settlers were not happy with the new British policies. The French had been generous to the Indians with their trade goods in order to compete with the British for furs. They often traded weapons and gunpowder for pelts. The British felt offering expensive trade goods was no longer necessary. There was no need to compete with other traders. Nor did they continue to offer guns and gunpowder. The British were worried about what the Indians might do with the weapons.

The Indians were insulted by these changes. They were also concerned about the British takeover of forts and trading posts. The French had never been very populous. As a result, white settlers were of little concern to the Indians. But the British posed another situation altogether. They far outnumbered the French. The Indians grew worried about the number of whites who began making their way into Indian lands. In May 1763 the great Indian leader Pontiac led a revolt against the British. Hundreds died before the British army squashed the rebellion in 1764.[2]

The French were also unhappy with some British policies. They preferred their own customs of religion, land ownership, and local government.

These events, combined with growing unrest in the thirteen American colonies, troubled the British. They were afraid that the French settlers in Quebec might join the colonies in a revolution against them.

Chief Pontiac fought with the French during the French and Indian War. After the French and Indians were defeated, Pontiac continued attacks on the British in response to their changes in trade policy. He was murdered by another Indian in 1769.

They realized they needed to make some changes.

The British passed a new statute to correct some of these problems. The Quebec Act of 1774 extended Quebec's official boundaries to include the Great Lakes and the Ohio River Valley. It reinstated the popular landholding policies of New France. It also softened its position on religious and political issues to the benefit of the French citizens.[3]

The Act came just in time. The American colonies launched the American Revolution against the British in April 1775. Quebec refused to join the Americans, though some secretly hoped that the Americans would win. In that case, the British might be driven out and the French could retake Quebec.

Soon after the outbreak of the war, American forces moved north. They captured British forts all the way to Montreal. Attacking Quebec City in late December, the American army held it under siege for more than six months.

Quebec Act extends Quebec's official boundaries
1763
1775–1783
1774
Britain gains most of New France; Ottawa Chief Pontiac wages war against the British
American Revolution

The British navy moved into the St. Lawrence River the following spring. They brought much-needed troops and supplies to Quebec City and broke the siege. The Americans retreated. They would make no further attempt to invade Canada.

The other major action involving Quebec came the following year. A body of British troops moved south to attack the American colonists. The campaign ended in a humiliating defeat at Saratoga.[4]

The balance of the revolution took place without involving Quebec much. Small forces raided the American frontier until the Americans gained the upper hand in 1779. Actual fighting in the war ended with the British surrender at Yorktown, Virginia, in 1781. The Americans hoped to gain Quebec as part of the peace agreement in 1783, but were disappointed. No major changes in territory took place. The boundary changed only slightly, to nearly its present position between Maine and the Great Lakes.[5]

Although the borders remained the same, the population changed dramatically. Loyalists (sometimes called Tories) were American colonists who chose to remain loyal to England during the Revolutionary War. A few moved to Canada during the war. That trickle turned into a flood when the war was over. According to estimates, somewhere between 30,000 and 50,000 Loyalists moved north at that time. Most moved to Nova Scotia. There were so many that a new province was created in 1784: New Brunswick.[6] A much smaller number settled outside of Quebec City.

The new colonists were not used to some of the French customs that were still common there. They did not like the system of colonial government or land ownership. The British government came up with

New Brunswick is created from part of Nova Scotia
1783
1791
North West Company founded
1784
Constitutional Act (Canada Act) divides Canada into Upper Canada and Lower Canada

HUDSON'S BAY COMPANY.

The Hudson's Bay Company was established in 1670. It controlled the fur trade in British North America for hundreds of years. In 1869 it sold its territory to the newly created Dominion of Canada, greatly increasing Canada's size.

a plan called the Constitutional Act of 1791 that they hoped would make both sides happy. The Act divided Quebec into Upper Canada and Lower Canada. This was the first use of "Canada" as an official name.

The division was both geographical and cultural. Upper Canada (now Ontario) consisted of lands west of the Ottawa River. Most inhabitants were English. Lower Canada (now Quebec) was east of this line. The majority of its inhabitants were of French descent. Lower Canada

1763
Britain gains most of New France; Ottawa Chief Pontiac wages war against the British
1774
Quebec Act extends Quebec's official boundaries
1775–1783
American Revolution

has maintained many of the French customs and laws that had been in existence since the founding of New France.[7]

The division of Canada into two provinces did not work. It only strengthened the differences between English and French. The two groups disagreed about how the government made decisions, how

Prior to confederation in 1867, British Canada was concentrated in and around the St. Lawrence River and its source, the Great Lakes. The St. Lawrence remains a vital means of transportation, trade, and industry to both Canada and the United States.

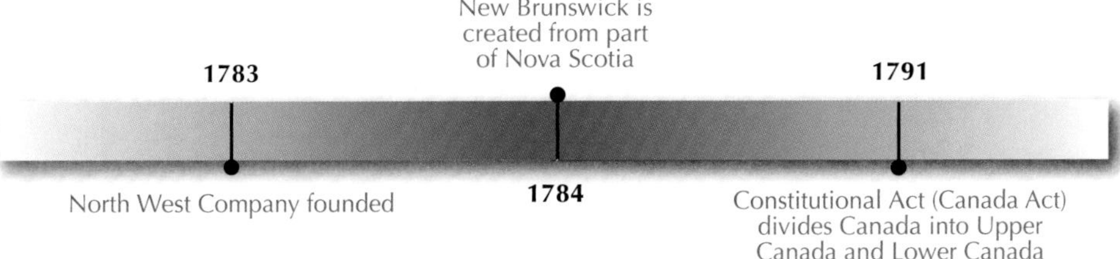

money was distributed, even how the people were represented in government. Riots broke out in the late 1830s. The territory was in chaos.

The British decided there was only one answer: to reunite the provinces. In 1840 the Act of Union joined Upper and Lower Canada in one province, the Province of Canada. English became the official language, and British government rules and structures were put into place. While the Act of Union solved some of the problems governing the territory, it was very unpopular with the French Canadians. They resented how they had been treated. By 1848 they forced the acceptance of French as an official language.

While these events took place in the east, the fur trade continued in the west. As had been the case for more than a hundred years, the British competed with the French. The British Hudson's Bay Company had been dominant in the northern area known as Rupert's Land since its founding in 1670. The French voyageurs meanwhile continued their intrepid exploration of western lands.

In the 1780s the French founded a rival trading company known as the North West Company. Over the next forty years, its representatives founded forts and trading posts from the Great Lakes to the Pacific Ocean.[8]

The North West Company was especially interested in the two great rivers of the Northwest, the Columbia and the Fraser. For a time it was hoped the Columbia River would become the southern border with the United States. But many Americans also lived in that area. The Oregon Treaty of 1846 set the boundary at the 49th parallel, much farther north. This meant less territory for Canada.

To avoid losing more territory to the United States, the Canadian government established a crown colony on Vancouver Island in 1849.

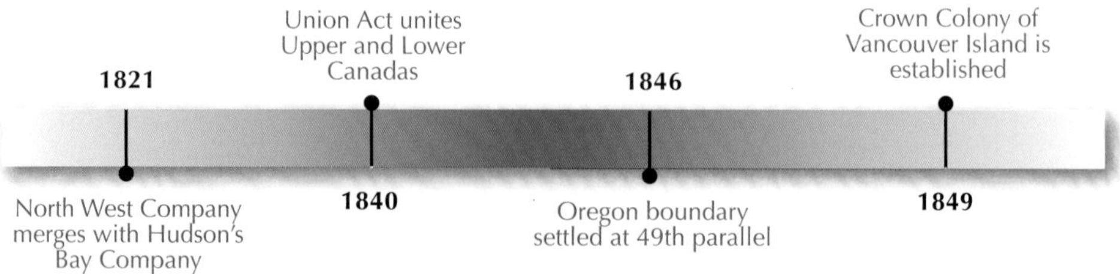
1821
North West Company merges with Hudson's Bay Company
1840
Union Act unites Upper and Lower Canadas
1846
Oregon boundary settled at 49th parallel
1849
Crown Colony of Vancouver Island is established

A crown colony was a way of staking a Canadian claim on an area. This was an effective strategy. In 1858, when news of the discovery of gold in the Fraser River reached the United States, thousands of American miners poured into the area. The British rushed to create another crown colony in British Columbia and were successful in keeping that territory once the rush was over.

As these events developed on the western frontier, a new threat loomed for the eastern provinces. In 1861 the American Civil War

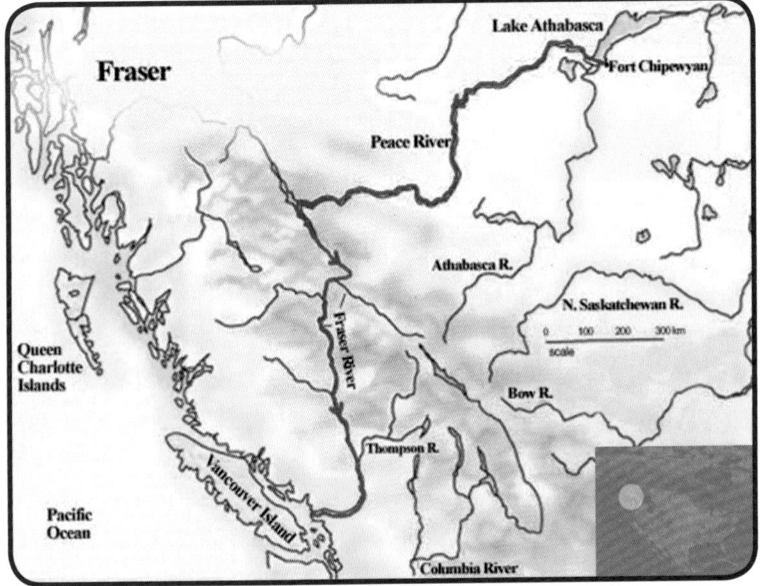

Vancouver Island sits off the west coast of Canada and the United States. Vancouver Island and British Columbia emerged as population centers as a result of the Fraser River Gold Rush. Canada used its crown colony system to keep the lands from being taken over by the United States.

broke out. As the conflict raged, millions of Americans became soldiers. American troops far outnumbered Canadian militia. Once the war was over, they could have posed a dangerous threat to Canada. Any help from the British would be a long time in coming, perhaps too late to help.[9]

An 1869 illustration of the Battle of Ridgeway near Ridgeway, Canada West (currently Ontario). The battle took place on June 2, 1866, between Canadian troops (left) and an Irish-American army called the Fenians. The Fenians wanted to overthrow British rule in Canada. Because the Canadians had been prepared for an invasion by U.S. forces, they easily repelled the Fenians. The Canadians kept their land.

For more than one hundred years Canadians had worried about what the Americans called Manifest Destiny. Manifest Destiny described some Americans' desire to control the entire North American continent. Canadians were keenly aware of this desire. After the American Revolution, they watched as the United States spread across the continent. Originally a small cluster of colonies hugging the Atlantic coast, the United States had gobbled up the western frontier until it reached the Pacific. What had begun as thirteen states after the American Revolution quickly grew to thirty-six states plus several territories by the end of the Civil War. With the purchase of Alaska from Russia in 1867, the Americans appeared to be interested in the only free land left within easy reach: Canada.

The Canadian Gold Rush

The fur trade was the foundation for the exploration and settlement of Canada. It made a tremendous amount of money for many people. In 1858 a new way to make money was discovered in the Fraser River: gold.

When a ship landed in San Francisco in 1858 bearing some of the Fraser River gold, thousands of men flocked to British Columbia to seek their fortunes. They came by land and sea. The water route through the city of Victoria on Vancouver Island was easier, but took longer. Many miners took the overland route to save time. Narrow trails meandered along cliffs and through muddy swamps. Towns sprang up overnight to feed and house the miners. Roads were built.

At the beginning of the rush, much gold was found in the river and creek beds. Gold is heavy. It sinks if it is dislodged from the rock that contains it and falls into the river, where it accumulates in the bends and curves.

The miners used simple equipment to look for gold. The most basic tool was a metal pan. The miner knelt in the creek in an area that looked like it might be a good spot to find some gold. He used his pan to scoop some gravel and rocks from the river bottom. When he gently swirled the water around in his pan, the lighter materials washed away and the heavier rocks stayed in the pan. Sometimes the heavy rocks glittered. Gold!

A man pans for gold

Miners could use other equipment to find more gold faster than they could with a pan. They built long rectangular screened boxes, called sluices, and washed larger amounts of gravel in these. The heavier gold was left behind. Miners occasionally use both of these methods today.

The Fraser Gold Rush faded in 1860, but it led to other rushes farther north in British Columbia. Millions of dollars' worth of gold were mined there in the next century. Gold is still mined in Canada. New sources are discovered every year.[10]

The thirteen provinces and territories of Canada stretch from sea to sea. Canada is the second-largest nation in the world. It extends through six time zones and has a population of more than 32 million people.

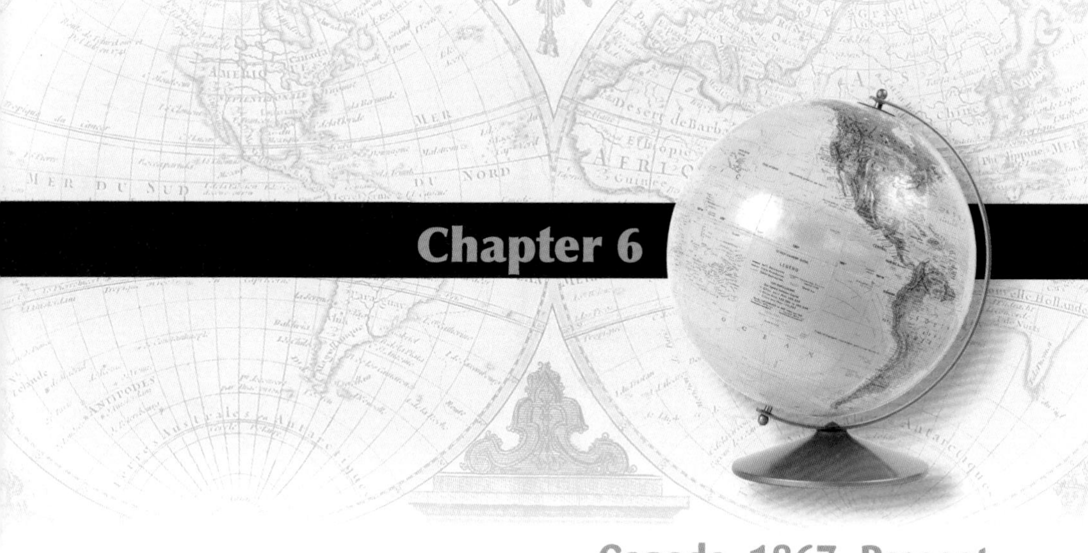

Chapter 6

Canada, 1867–Present

The best solution to the perceived threat to Canada from the United States seemed to be *confederation*, or joining the Canadian provinces together. After much discussion, the British North America Act was passed by the English House of Lords in 1867. The four provinces of Upper Canada, Lower Canada, Nova Scotia, and New Brunswick were now known as The Dominion of Canada.[1] Though Newfoundland and Prince Edward Island chose not to join at that time, it was the first step in creating a nation that would stretch from the Atlantic to the Pacific.

In order to protect its claim on the lands in western Canada, Canada began its own program of westward expansion. Its leaders longed to spread across the continent before the hordes of Americans got there. The strategy was simple: stake a claim to the land with settlers, business, soldiers, or some combination. Then provide benefits such as railroads to convince the inhabitants to join the Dominion. Or, as was the case of the Hudson's Bay Company, the government could buy the land outright.

Almost immediately after confederation, the Canadian government entered talks with the Hudson's Bay Company to purchase Rupert's Land. These lands stretched from Hudson Bay to the Arctic Circle, then west almost to the Pacific, butting up against Alaska. By 1869 the Dominion of Canada had acquired one and a half million square miles of land in what was now named the Northwest Territories. Similar to the Louisiana Purchase* by the United States in 1803, the deal with

*See Chapter 7.

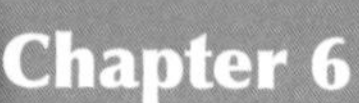

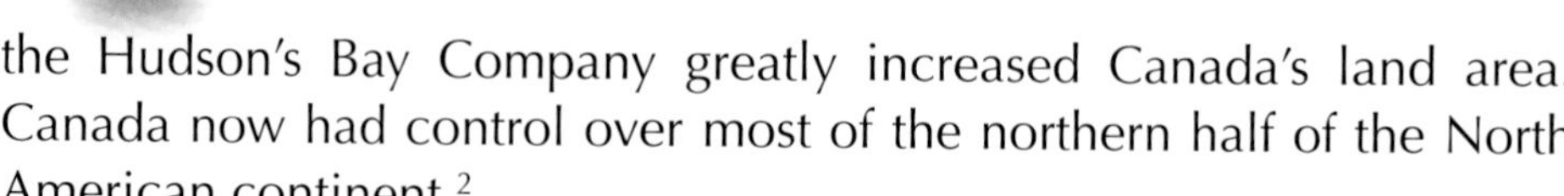

the Hudson's Bay Company greatly increased Canada's land area. Canada now had control over most of the northern half of the North American continent.[2]

RIEL

Louis Riel was a Canadian politician, a founder of the province of Manitoba, and leader of the Métis people.

Manitoba became the first new province after confederation. When Canada purchased Rupert's Land, settlers rushed to its fertile plains. The arrival of these newcomers disrupted the fur trading communities along the Red River near today's Winnipeg. The native populations, French-speaking traders, and mixed-blood peoples known as Métis (MAY-teez) had lived in the area for decades. They resented not being consulted when Canada purchased the territory. The Manitoba Act of 1870 was designed to address their concerns. It created the province of Manitoba. Originally Manitoba was only about 100 miles long on each side, about five percent of its current extent. Nicknamed "the postage stamp province"[3] at that time, Manitoba became increasingly larger and finally reached its present size in 1912.

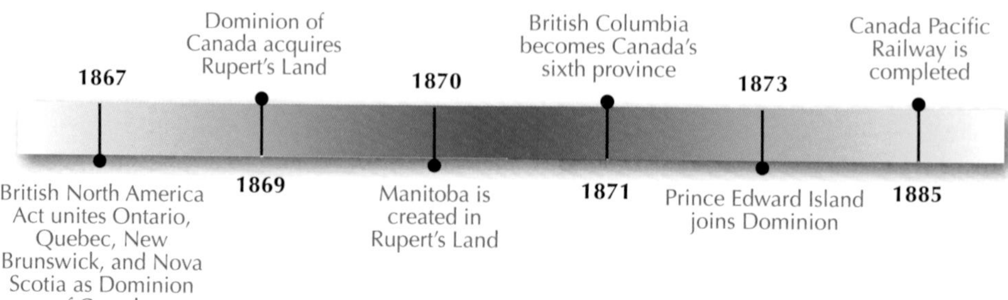
1867
British North America Act unites Ontario, Quebec, New Brunswick, and Nova Scotia as Dominion of Canada
1869
Dominion of Canada acquires Rupert's Land
1870
Manitoba is created in Rupert's Land
1871
British Columbia becomes Canada's sixth province
1873
Prince Edward Island joins Dominion
1885
Canada Pacific Railway is completed

British Columbia was next to join. With more Americans coming to Oregon to the south and the recent purchase of Alaska to the northwest, Americans could begin putting pressure on the British Columbia settlements. Becoming part of Canada would eliminate this problem, so British Columbia became the sixth province in 1871. Prince Edward Island reversed its original position and joined the Dominion in 1873.[4]

The Klondike Gold Rush, which began with the discovery of the precious metal in the remote Yukon River in 1896, brought thousands of fortune seekers to the snowbound wilderness of the Canadian northwest. In order to keep the area under Canadian control, the Yukon was carved out of the Northwest Territories and made a separate territory in 1898.[5]

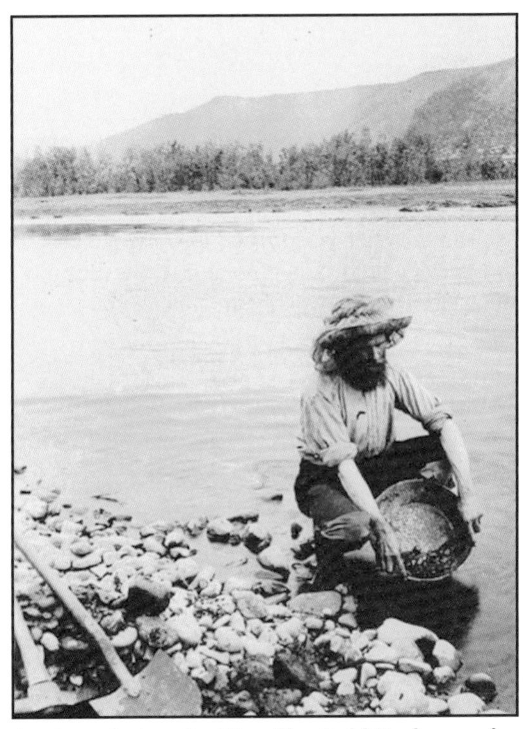

A miner during the Klondike Gold Rush pans for gold. The miner swirls river water around in his pan. The heavier gold nuggets will sink to the bottom.

The open prairies of Canada had a different kind of gold: wheat. When the United States eliminated the settlement of public lands in 1896, thousands of immigrants hungry for cheap land poured into Canada's western plains. They

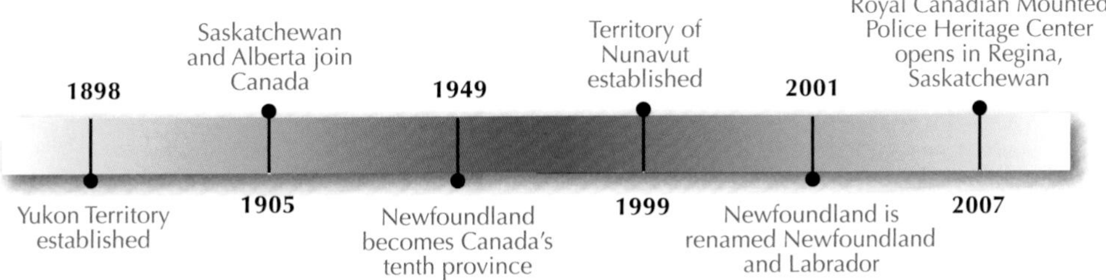
1898
Yukon Territory established
1905
Saskatchewan and Alberta join Canada
1949
Newfoundland becomes Canada's tenth province
1999
Territory of Nunavut established
2001
Newfoundland is renamed Newfoundland and Labrador
2007
Royal Canadian Mounted Police Heritage Center opens in Regina, Saskatchewan

Miners also used sluices, or troughs of water, to mine for gold. The wooden sluices moved much more water than panning, but the principal was the same. Water was forced into the sluices, and the heavier gold nuggets sank to the bottom as the water flowed over them.

were delighted to find that certain types of wheat grew that far north. By 1905 the population had increased dramatically. That year, Alberta and Saskatchewan became Canada's eighth and ninth provinces. The completion of the Canadian Pacific Railway in 1885 also contributed greatly to the population of the western prairies.[6]

Throughout the twentieth century, Canada experienced few changes to its territorial boundaries. But it continued to grow in other ways. It developed a highly skilled military. French Canadians in particular had a strong military tradition going back to the times of New France. Canadian forces fought valiantly in World Wars I and II. Their successes brought attention and respect to the young country.[7]

The 1930s were a time of hardship and despair in both the cities and the farms across Canada. The Great Depression hit Canada as well as the United States. Drought, wind, and grasshoppers destroyed crops. Markets for farm and manufactured goods dried up. People lost their jobs. The government offered public assistance when possible. At last, the economy turned around with the start of World War II.[8]

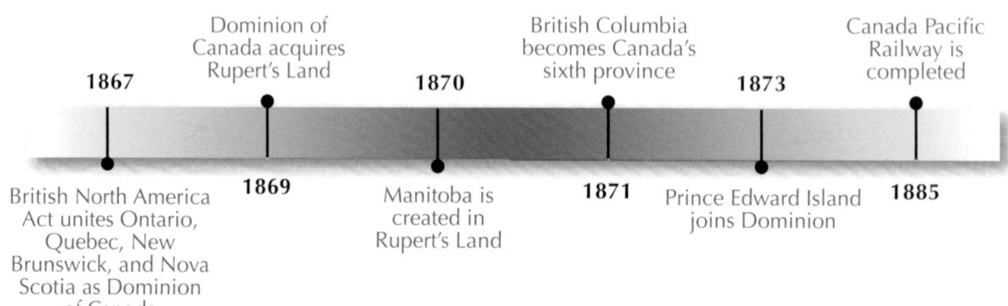
1867
British North America Act unites Ontario, Quebec, New Brunswick, and Nova Scotia as Dominion of Canada
1869
Dominion of Canada acquires Rupert's Land
1870
Manitoba is created in Rupert's Land
1871
British Columbia becomes Canada's sixth province
1873
Prince Edward Island joins Dominion
1885
Canada Pacific Railway is completed

In 1949 the province of Newfoundland joined the Dominion. It was renamed Newfoundland and Labrador in 2001.[9]

The most recent adjustment to the Canadian map occurred in 1999. Nunavut Territory was created from more than 700,000 square miles of Northwest Territories land.[10] It extends north and east from the Northwest Territories, curving around the north end of Hudson Bay. It is the largest of all the territories and provinces in Canada. Most of its inhabitants are Inuit. These native peoples have lived in Canada for more than four thousand years.

The Canadian Pacific Railway was completed in 1885. It connected eastern Canada with British Columbia. The railroad was a major factor in bringing settlers to western Canada.

If the founders of New France could see their land today, what would they think? They arrived searching for a route to China. A route was eventually discovered, but it took almost four hundred years to find it. And it was nowhere near where anyone had imagined it would be. In 1906 Norwegian explorer Roald Amundsen sailed over the top of Canada from the Atlantic to the Pacific. However, the icy seas are too treacherous to use as a practical trading route.[11]

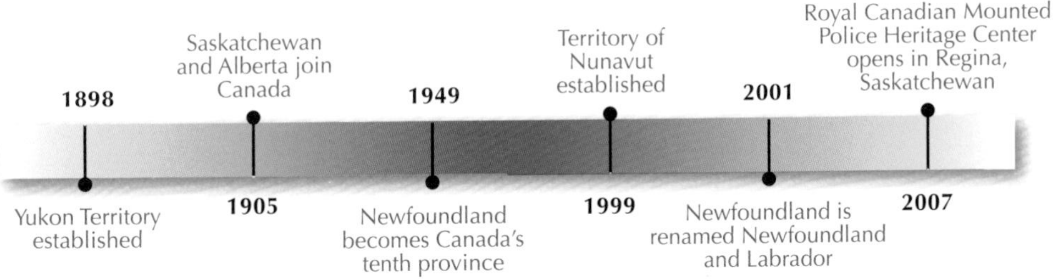
1898
Yukon Territory established
Saskatchewan and Alberta join Canada
1905
1949
Newfoundland becomes Canada's tenth province
Territory of Nunavut established
1999
2001
Newfoundland is renamed Newfoundland and Labrador
Royal Canadian Mounted Police Heritage Center opens in Regina, Saskatchewan
2007

Chapter 6

The Nunavut Territory was created from part of the Northwest Territories in 1999. It is the largest province/territory in Canada, perched along the icy waters of Hudson Bay and the Arctic Ocean. The territory was established as a homeland for the native Inuit peoples. The Inuit depend on the land for furs, food, and shelter.

1867 — British North America Act unites Ontario, Quebec, New Brunswick, and Nova Scotia as Dominion of Canada

1869

Dominion of Canada acquires Rupert's Land — 1870

Manitoba is created in Rupert's Land — 1871

British Columbia becomes Canada's sixth province — 1873

Prince Edward Island joins Dominion

Canada Pacific Railway is completed — 1885

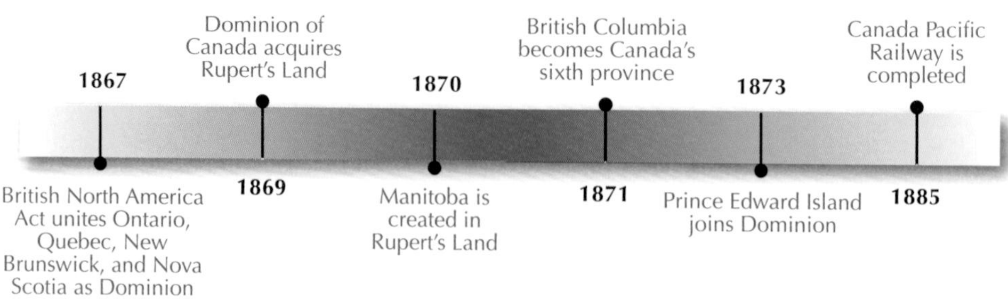

In 1906, Norwegian explorer Roald Amundsen became the first to successfully sail from the Atlantic to the Pacific Ocean via a northern passage. The journey took three years. Because of weather and water conditions, the Northwest Passage was considered impractical for use as a trade route.

French explorers also hoped to find gold, silver, and spices. While Canada is rich in mineral resources, gold and silver weren't discovered until the 1800s. Gold and silver mines are still in operation today. As for spices, the French didn't find pepper, cinnamon, or ginger. The climate is too cold to grow them. However, wheat has become Canada's most important crop. Canada grows much more wheat than it needs for itself. Much of this extra wheat is sold to other countries, making it an important part of the Canadian economy.[12]

The mighty beaver, source of wealth and the reason for the great French explorations, is still around. The animals almost died out during the fur trade era, but they were saved by the silk hat. In the 1800s, people started wearing silk hats instead of fur. The fur trapping industry faded away, but not the beaver. Today the beaver population is alive and well in Canada.[13]

Even the most optimistic Frenchman could not have imagined that New France would one day become the foundation for one of the

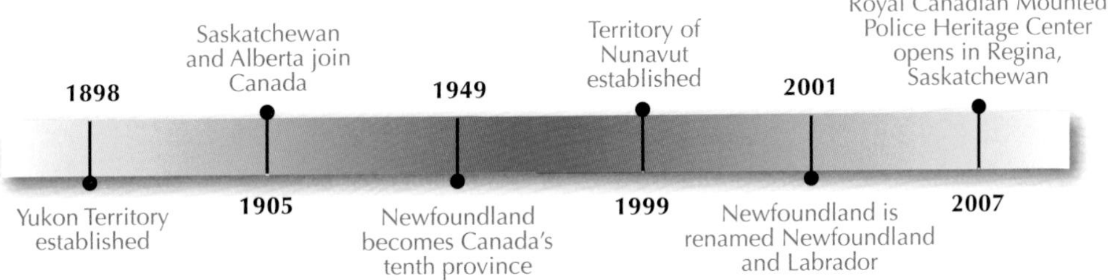

The beaver played an important role in the history of the exploration and settlement of much of North America. While they live in lakes and streams, beavers can also be found on the official seal of the City of New York, on the logo of the Canadian Pacific Railway, and serving as mascot for scores of sports teams across both Canada and the United States. The beaver is one of Canada's official emblems.

largest countries in the world. Canada is second only to Russia in size, covering nearly four million square miles. Quite impressive, considering it all began with a few French fishermen hoping to dry and salt their cod on the rocky shores of Newfoundland.

For Your Information

The Mounties

A modern-day Mountie

With their brilliant red jackets and crisp tan Stetson hats, the Royal Canadian Mounted Police, or Mounties, are one of Canada's most recognizable symbols. The Mounties are Canada's federal police force. With more than 23,000 members, they are the country's largest police force.

The Mounties were founded by Canada's first prime minister, John A. Macdonald, in 1873. Macdonald based the North-West Mounted Police, as they were first known, on the British military structure. They were called "mounted" because the entire unit was on horseback; no foot soldiers were included. The uniforms with their distinctive red jackets were similar to those of the British, who were sometimes called "redcoats" during the American Revolution. At first, the Mounties wore either flat, round hats or white pith helmets. These hats were soon replaced with the more practical Stetson, a type of cowboy hat.

Macdonald didn't waste any time using the Mounties. In 1874 he sent the first patrol to Alberta to deal with trouble caused by American whiskey traders. This "March West" consisted of more than 250 men and their horses, plus weapons and supplies. They were determined to bring law and order to the frontier.

They succeeded. Soon they were needed again. They helped keep the peace during the Klondike Gold Rush. The Mounties also served in foreign conflicts. They fought in the South African War (1899–1902) and World Wars I and II. In 1920 they merged with Canada's Dominion Police and were renamed the Royal Canadian Mounted Police (RCMP).

Today Mounties serve many roles in Canada. They enforce Canadian federal laws. They also provide police services for many provinces, cities, and towns. The Mounties protect government officials. They are like the American Secret Service, National Guard, FBI, and police, all rolled into one.

The Mounties honor their heritage with an event known as the Musical Ride. During the Musical Ride, thirty-two RCMP officers demonstrate their horsemanship with complex formations and drills performed to music. The Musical Ride is performed at a variety of locations throughout Canada.[14]

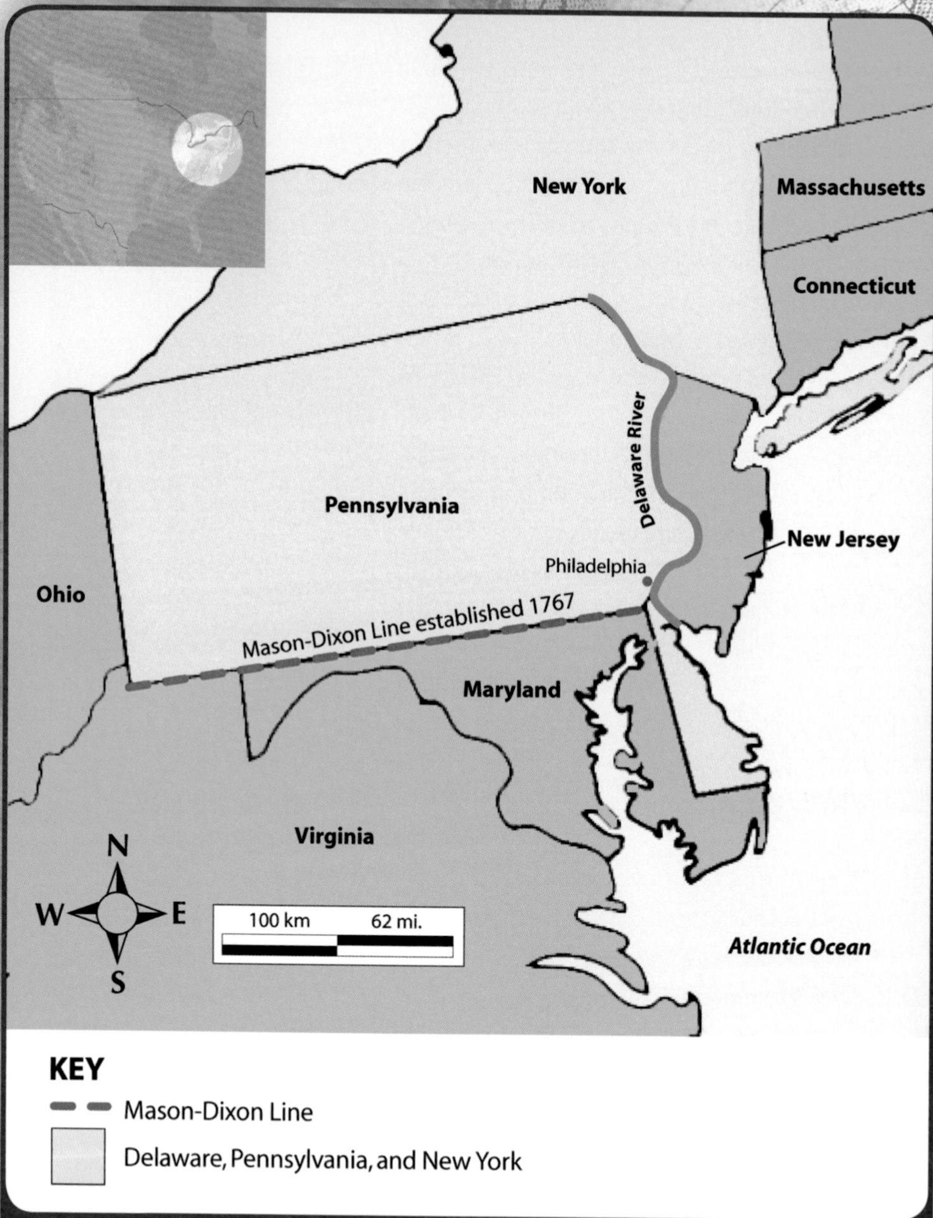

With the British capture of New Amsterdam in 1664, New Netherland and New Sweden were quickly absorbed into the British American colonial system. Both became parts of much larger colonies. New Netherland was surrounded by the lands known as New York. New Sweden's settlements along the Delaware River were in the Pennsylvania and New Jersey colonies.

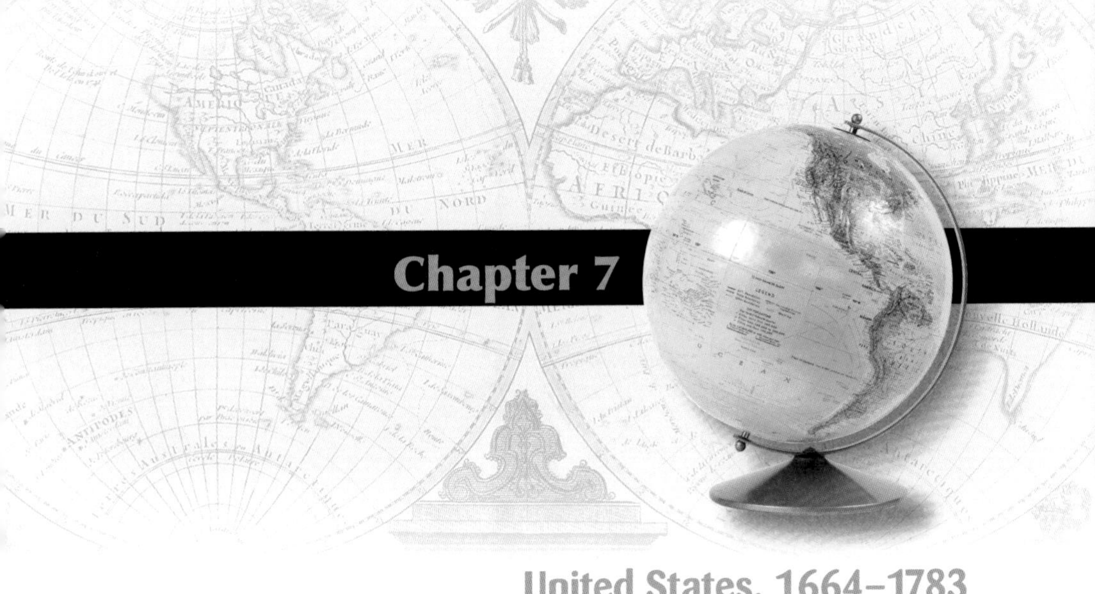

Chapter 7

United States, 1664–1783

When Peter Stuyvesant surrendered New Amsterdam to the British in 1664, New Netherland and New Sweden became part of the large land grant that belonged to James, the Duke of York.

Daily life remained the same. Swedes, Finns, and Dutch remained on their farms and at their businesses. They tilled the land and hunted deer and turkey for their dinner. They traded with the Lenapes and Mohawks, and sold furs to the trading companies as they always had.

They acquired a new neighbor in 1681. King Charles II granted a huge tract of land to an Englishman named William Penn. Located south of New York and west of the Delaware River, it was about the same size as the entire country of England.[1] At the king's suggestion, Penn named it Pennsylvania after his father.

William Penn was a Quaker. Quakers were a religious group that was not welcome in England. Penn hoped to settle his colony with other Quakers. He also planned a new city, Philadelphia, to serve as its capital. The site had been part of New Sweden, though the Swedes hadn't established any settlements there.

The new colony had one big problem: It was landlocked. There was no easy access to the Atlantic Ocean. So Penn leased more land from the Duke of York in 1682. The added territory included three counties bordering Delaware Bay. Much of this land had formerly been part of New Sweden. These counties, known as the Lower Counties, became a separate territory under the Pennsylvania Colony.[2]

Chapter 7

Under pressure from the residents of New Amsterdam, Governor Peter Stuyvesant surrenders to the British in 1664. The city was quickly renamed New York. Stuyvesant used a wooden leg to replace the one he lost in a battle in the Caribbean.

The population of the American colonies grew quickly after 1700. Settlers edged closer to the western borders of each colony. Disputes arose over hunting and trading rights. In the 1750s, trouble brewed between France and England with the outbreak of the French and Indian War.* Some battles took place in the old Dutch fur trading territory of upstate New York, north of Albany. When the war ended in 1763, the British did not want any more conflicts with the Indians.

*See Chapter 2.

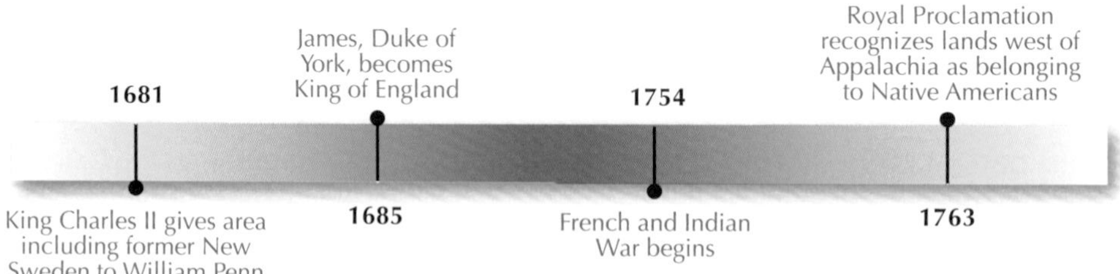
1681
King Charles II gives area including former New Sweden to William Penn
1685
James, Duke of York, becomes King of England
1754
French and Indian War begins
1763
Royal Proclamation recognizes lands west of Appalachia as belonging to Native Americans

William Penn greets inhabitants of his new colony, Pennsylvania. Part of Pennsylvania along the Delaware River had formerly been New Sweden. During the American Revolution part of it would be transferred to the state of Delaware.

Before the war, the British colonies had sometimes been granted without western boundaries. They could stretch on forever! According to the Royal Proclamation of 1763, all lands west of the Appalachian Mountains now belonged to the Indians who already lived there. Only the British government could make treaties to buy Indian land. The western border of the American colonies became a squiggly line on a map, running through the middle of the Appalachian Mountains. Settlers had to stay on the east side of that line.

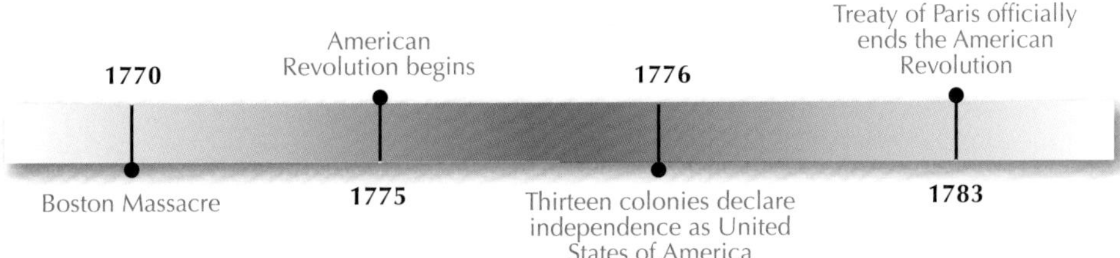
1770
Boston Massacre
American Revolution begins
1775
1776
Thirteen colonies declare independence as United States of America
Treaty of Paris officially ends the American Revolution
1783

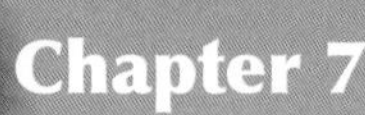

Many colonists resented the Proclamation. They didn't like how it limited the establishment of new settlements. Meanwhile, the British thought that the colonies should help pay for the high cost of fighting the French and Indian War. To raise money, the English government passed the Sugar Act in 1764 and the Stamp Act in 1765.

Relations quickly grew frosty between England and its American colonies. The Sugar and Stamp Acts were a form of taxation. Many colonists didn't think it was fair to be taxed if they didn't get to vote on the matter.

The more the colonists protested, the harder England tried to enforce order. British soldiers in their red jackets became a common sight in the major cities. The colonists, who had been grateful for the British army's exploits in the French and Indian War, now viewed the soldiers with disdain. Tensions built over the tax laws and the quartering laws (laws forcing colonists to house soldiers).

In 1770, five colonists were killed in what became known as the Boston Massacre. Three years later a group of Bostonians dressed as Indians dumped 324 containers of tea into Boston Harbor rather than pay taxes on it.[3] For the British, the "Boston Tea Party" was the last straw. They passed more laws to bring the colonists under control.

Many colonists disliked the new laws. In 1774 the First Continental Congress met in Philadelphia to discuss how to respond. Militias began training. In April 1775, British troops were ordered to Concord, Massachusetts, to destroy some weapons the colonists had stored there. Local colonists stood ready to defend it. They had been warned by Paul Revere during his famous ride that the British were coming. Colonists confronted the British troops at Lexington, seven miles from Concord. Shots rang out. The American Revolution had begun.

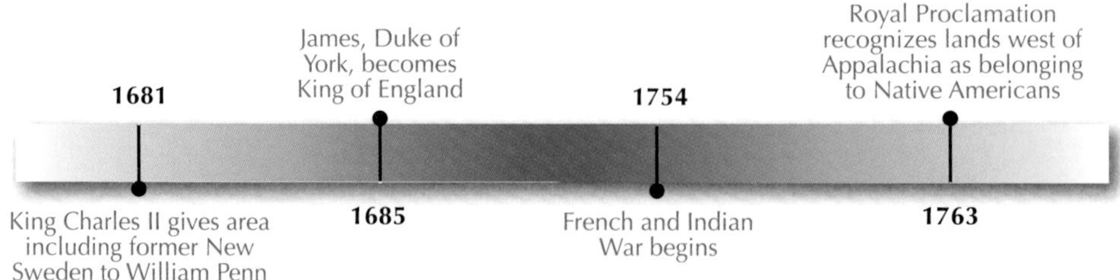

After the skirmishes at Lexington and Concord, the Continental Congress met again in Philadelphia. It elected George Washington as general and commander in chief of the Continental Army. In June 1775 the first official battle of the Revolutionary War was waged at Bunker Hill near Boston.

In July 1776 the Continental Congress approved the Declaration of Independence in Philadelphia. Soon afterward, individual colonies created their own governments. The Lower Counties declared their own independence from Pennsylvania and gave themselves a new name. The former New Sweden was now known as Delaware.[4]

The Battle of Bunker Hill took place in 1775 during the American Revolution. American colonists rebelled against taxation and other policies forced upon them by the British.

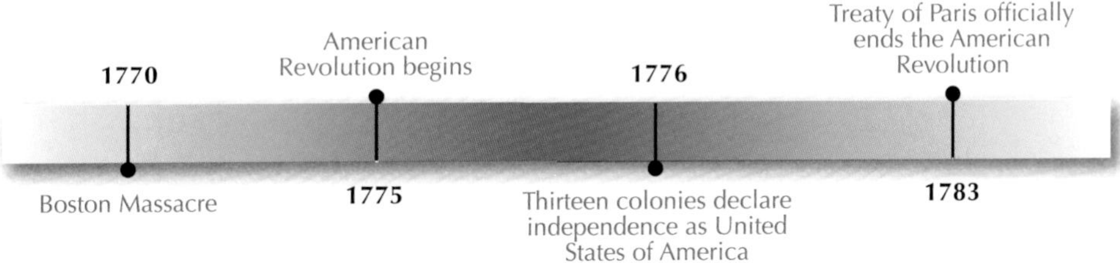
1770
Boston Massacre
American Revolution begins
1775
1776
Thirteen colonies declare independence as United States of America
Treaty of Paris officially ends the American Revolution
1783

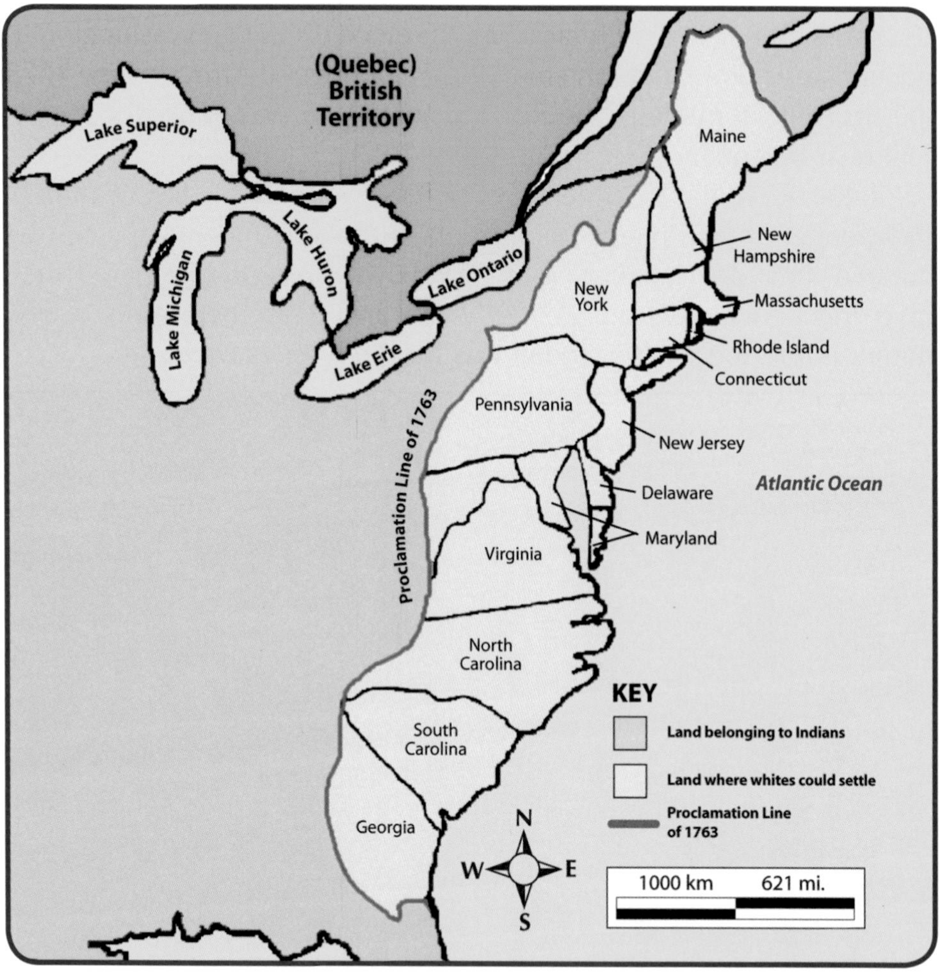

Chapter 7

(Quebec) British Territory
Lake Superior
Lake Michigan
Lake Huron
Lake Ontario
Lake Erie
Proclamation Line of 1763
Maine
New Hampshire
Massachusetts
Rhode Island
Connecticut
New York
Pennsylvania
New Jersey
Delaware
Maryland
Virginia
North Carolina
South Carolina
Georgia
Atlantic Ocean
KEY
Land belonging to Indians
Land where whites could settle
Proclamation Line of 1763
N
W
E
S
1000 km
621 mi.

The Royal Proclamation of 1763 attempted to improve relations with the Indians living along the western frontier of the American colonies. White settlement on lands west of the proclamation line was outlawed. Only the British government could legally purchase lands from the Indians.

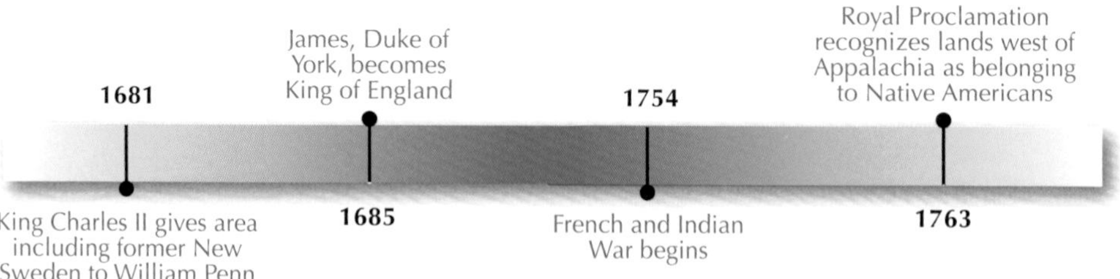
1681
King Charles II gives area including former New Sweden to William Penn
James, Duke of York, becomes King of England
1685
1754
French and Indian War begins
Royal Proclamation recognizes lands west of Appalachia as belonging to Native Americans
1763

Delaware quickly organized the Delaware Continentals to fight in the war. They served for seven years, longer than any other colonial regiment, and fought in every major battle.[5]

Revolutionary times were hard on the former New Netherland, now New York. Many battles occurred in upstate New York, lands formerly controlled by Dutch traders. The British moved troops south from Canada to fight at Lake Champlain and Albany. Indian raids were common on the western frontier as the Iroquois fought for their British allies.[6]

New York City had many Loyalists. Loyalists clashed often with patriots, those who wanted independence from England. When the colonies declared independence in 1776, thousands of Loyalists left. By July 1776 New York City's original population of 25,000 had dwindled to less than 5,000 residents.[7]

When the British army arrived in New York City, they had no trouble driving out the inexperienced American troops. Battles were fought in areas whose names reflected their Dutch roots: Harlem Heights, Brooklyn Heights, the Bronx. The British occupied New York City from 1776 until the end of the war in 1783.

Many Loyalists returned to New York City during the British occupation. They felt safer with the British army there. The army's presence and protection generated much business for New York City residents. The harbor was filled with ships. Many were privateers, licensed by the British government to prey on enemy ships and take their cargoes. The soldiers needed food, clothing, and supplies, which the residents were happy to supply at good prices.

Although the colonies had declared their independence, the Americans were outnumbered and undertrained. They struggled through

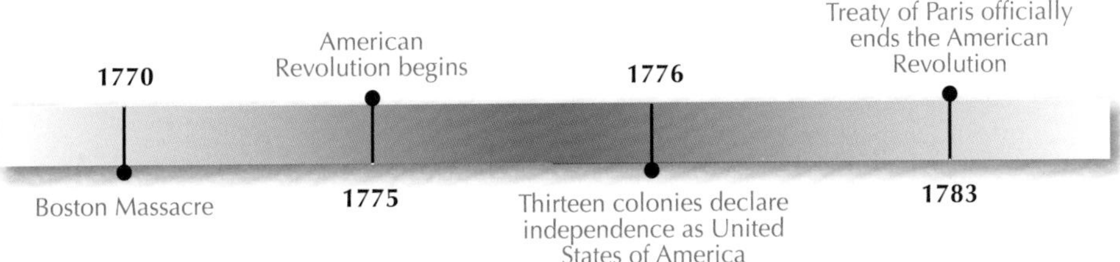
1770
Boston Massacre
American Revolution begins
1775
1776
Thirteen colonies declare independence as United States of America
Treaty of Paris officially ends the American Revolution
1783

The Americans won their independence in 1781 when British General Lord Cornwallis surrendered to George Washington (center) at Yorktown, Virginia. The two countries would be at war again during the War of 1812.

harsh winters with inadequate food and clothing. At first, the disciplined, well-supplied British Army won most of the battles.

Things changed in 1778. France pledged to help the Americans with ships, money, and supplies against its old enemy, England. In October 1781, American troops combined with French warships to surround the British General Lord Cornwallis at Yorktown, Virginia. Cornwallis surrendered and the fighting was over. The Treaty of Paris in 1783 officially ended the war. The thirteen British colonies were now an independent country, the United States of America.

The Pirates of New York

From the time of its founding by the Dutch, New York City was a beehive of business activity. Traders, shipbuilders, brewers, tailors, bakers, builders–the city had everything. Including pirates.

Pirates were businessmen, too. The ship's captain was his own boss. He owned his own ship. He hired (or kidnapped) his crew. The captain decided when and where to sail in search of his prey. Pirates roamed the shipping lanes, which were determined by currents and winds. When another ship came into view, the pirates went after it. They used speed, sailing skill, cannons and guns to stop the ship. Then they boarded it and took its cargo. When that was done, they towed the ship along with them or had their crew sail it. They might also burn or sink it.

A man dressed as the pirate Blackbeard

Pirates sometimes killed the crew of the captured ship, or they put them to work aboard their own ship. Around the world, pirates were hated and feared. They were considered criminals. If they were caught, they could be hanged.

There was another type of pirate called a *privateer*. Privateers also prowled the oceans looking for ships to capture. But privateers had the permission of their country to do so. Both sides used privateers extensively during the Revolutionary War.

Although authorized by the government, privateering was a business. Businessmen were happy to invest money with the privateer. In return, if the privateer was successful, the investors got to split the profits with him. Investing in privateers was considered a legitimate although risky business venture.

Captured ships weren't always loaded with gold and silver, but just about anything a ship carried could be sold for a profit. During the French and Indian war, privateers brought hundreds of captured ships into New York. They carried coffee, sugar, lumber, cotton, even slaves. Their cargoes made huge profits for their investors.[8]

States and Territories of the United States of America
April 30, 1803, to March 27, 1804

After the American colonies won independence from Britain, they wasted no time expanding their western borders. The acquisition of the Louisiana Territory from France in 1803 greatly increased the size of the young country. Settlers rushed west, eager for cheap land.

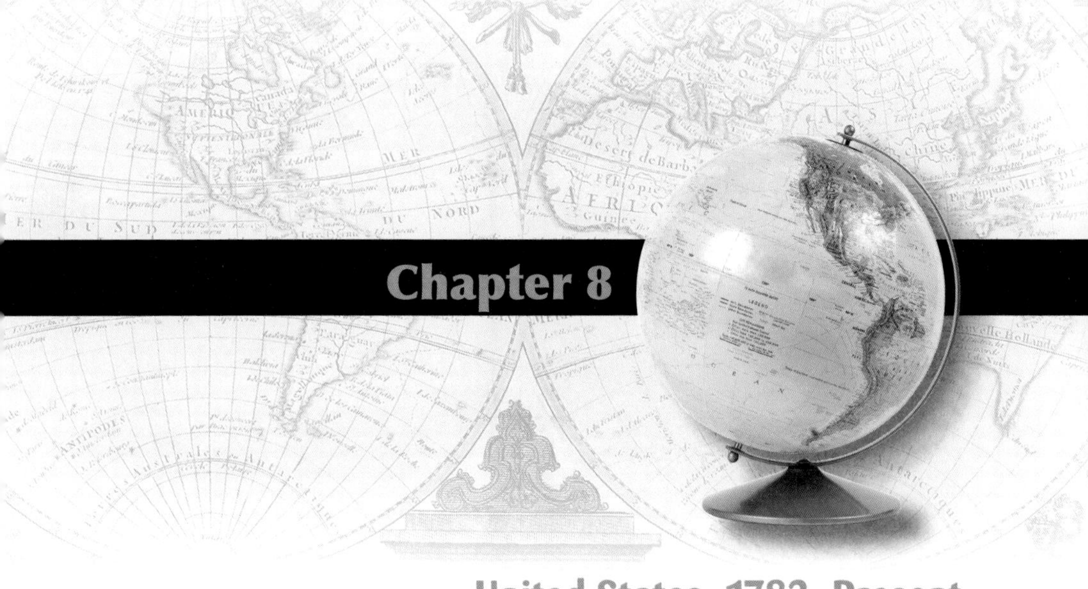

Chapter 8

United States, 1783–Present

When the American Revolution was over, the United States was a collection of thirteen former colonies clinging to the Atlantic coast. Over the next 125 years those thirteen colonies would grow to forty-eight states, stretching from the Atlantic to the Pacific. The addition of territory sometimes happened gradually. Other times it occurred almost overnight.

One result of the peace treaty with Britain was the extension of the western boundary of the United States. It would no longer stop at the 1763 proclamation line, but would go all the way to the Mississippi River. Several states were convinced to give their western lands to the government. Laws known as the Northwest Ordinances contained rules for turning these western lands into new states.[1]

By the 1780s the new country reworked some important aspects of its government. It had operated under a set of rules called the Articles of Confederation since 1777. But the Articles didn't work well. The states came to an agreement on a document known as the Constitution, which created a new form of government. It took effect in 1789. Delaware (once part of New Sweden) was the first state to ratify, or approve, the new Constitution. New York City, formerly New Amsterdam, sometimes served as the nation's capital during this time.

Thomas Jefferson became president of the United States in 1801. Jefferson dreamed of pushing the boundaries of the country farther to the west. Two years later, he bought the Louisiana Territory from the French emperor, Napoleon Bonaparte, for $15 million. The Louisiana

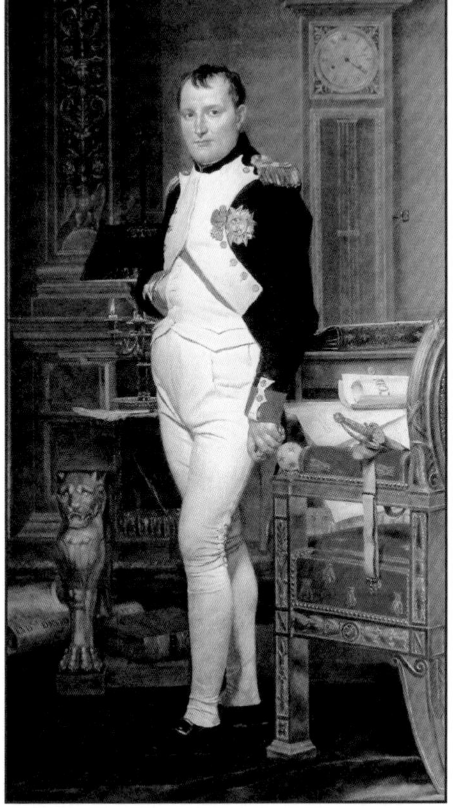

Napoleon Bonaparte, ruler of France. During his reign, France fought a lengthy war with England, which was partially responsible for the War of 1812 between the English and the United States. In 1803 Bonaparte agreed to sell Louisiana Territory to the United States for about 15 million dollars.

Purchase, as it became known, nearly doubled the area of the United States. It has been called "the greatest land deal in history."[2]

Jefferson sent Meriwether Lewis and William Clark to explore the new U.S. lands. It took the expedition more than two years to reach the Pacific and return.

The British also had dealings with Napoleon. These weren't so friendly. They had been at war with Napoleon and France since the final years of the eighteenth century. Desperate for sailors, the British repeatedly stopped American ships and forced crew members to join the British Navy. This was known as impressment.

The United States demanded that the British stop their impressment. When the British refused, war broke out in 1812 between the two countries. It was known as the War of 1812. Some Americans wanted to invade Canada and take it from the British.

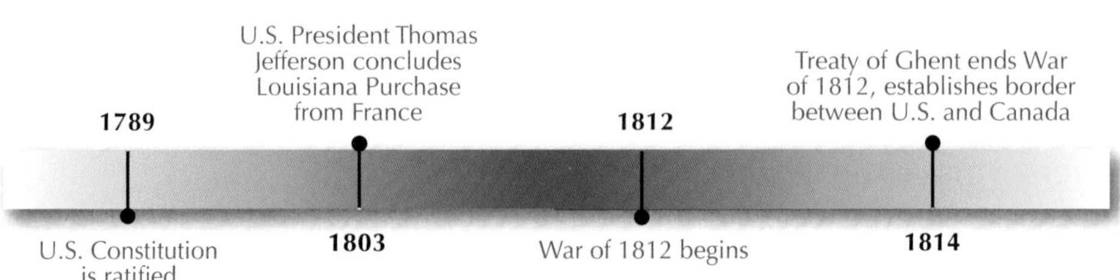
1789
U.S. Constitution is ratified
U.S. President Thomas Jefferson concludes Louisiana Purchase from France
1803
1812
War of 1812 begins
Treaty of Ghent ends War of 1812, establishes border between U.S. and Canada
1814

As in the French and Indian War and the American Revolution, many battles were fought on the western frontier. An Indian leader named Tecumseh fought with the British against the Americans. He hoped to drive American settlers out of Indian lands. Though he was killed in 1813, he is regarded as a hero in Canada because he helped defend Upper Canada from American invasion.

American forces struggled against the dual threat of the Indians on the frontier and the might of the British military at sea and on land. On the Atlantic coast, the British sailed up Chesapeake Bay in 1814 and marched into Washington, D.C. They set the city ablaze.

But as the war continued, British efforts crumbled. An invasion from Canada was turned back at the Battle of Plattsburgh (New York) on Lake Champlain.[3] Andrew Jackson defeated Indian and British forces in the south. The Treaty of Ghent, which both sides signed at the end of 1814, ended the war. The border between America and Canada remained as it had been before the war.

After the war of 1812 the westward expansion of America continued. Construction of the Erie Canal began in 1817. Its completion eight years later opened up an easy transportation route from the Great Lakes to the Hudson River and the Atlantic Ocean. It was no accident that the canal followed the same route the Dutch explorers took from the Hudson River west into Indian fur trading territory on the Great Lakes.[4]

By then the U.S. extended coast to coast as Americans began settling in Oregon Territory. In 1846 the Oregon border was placed at the 49th parallel (now the border of Washington State with Canada). The territory south of Oregon belonged to Mexico.

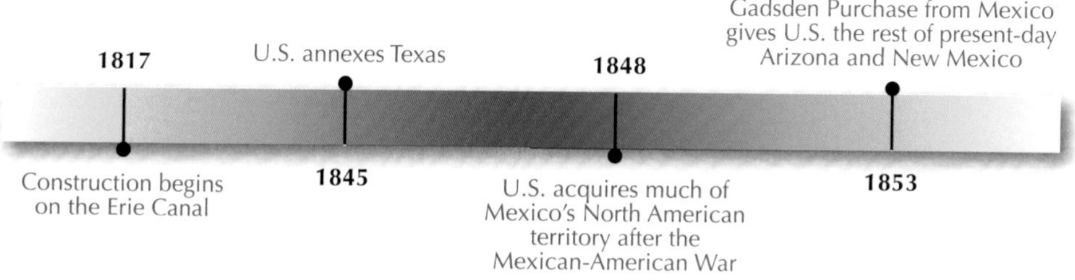
1817
Construction begins on the Erie Canal
1845
U.S. annexes Texas
1848
U.S. acquires much of Mexico's North American territory after the Mexican-American War
1853
Gadsden Purchase from Mexico gives U.S. the rest of present-day Arizona and New Mexico

The completion of the Erie Canal in New York State in 1825 connected the Great Lakes (Lake Erie) with the Hudson River. This new route simplified and reduced the cost of moving goods from the west to the Atlantic Ocean. The canal generally followed trails used by Dutch and Indian fur traders in the 1600s.

Mexico had broken away from Spain in 1821. It claimed all of Spain's territory in the New World. Mexico spanned Central America and up through the southern limits of the Louisiana Purchase. Part of this territory had broken away in 1836 and become the Republic of Texas. In 1845 Texas joined the United States as the twenty-eighth state. Mexico was angry. It refused to negotiate a border with Texas.

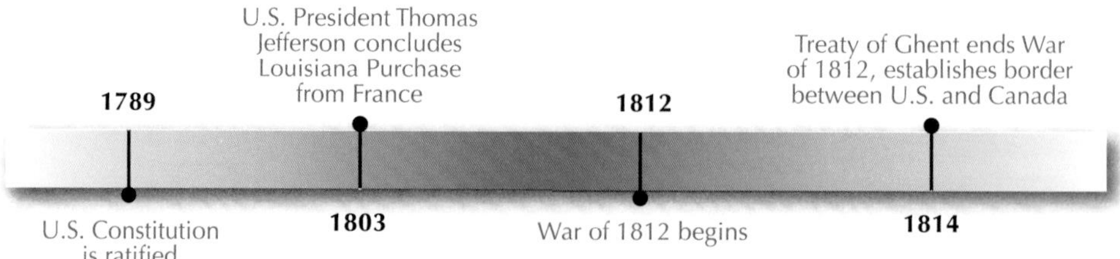
1789
U.S. Constitution is ratified
U.S. President Thomas Jefferson concludes Louisiana Purchase from France
1803
1812
War of 1812 begins
Treaty of Ghent ends War of 1812, establishes border between U.S. and Canada
1814

Relations between the two countries worsened. In 1846 hostilities broke out. The war with Mexico lasted until the Treaty of Guadalupe Hidalgo in 1848. The United States received all or parts of the future states of California, Arizona, New Mexico, Utah, Nevada and Colorado, and fixed the Texas-Mexico border at the Rio Grande.[5] The last bit of territory in Arizona and New Mexico to be filled in to create the current shape of the continental U.S. was acquired in the Gadsden Purchase of 1853.

While these territorial acquisitions were going on, the country was heading toward another war. During the march west, politicians argued over how best to administer this vast new territory. Foremost on their minds was the question of slavery. Should all new states allow slavery? Should none? The Compromise of 1850 was the answer, at least temporarily. It allowed each new state to decide for itself whether to allow slavery.

Slavery had been a controversial issue since the founding of the country. It existed everywhere, but as time passed, slavery became less common and less popular in the north. The majority of slaves were used in southern states. Northerners began insisting that slavery be outlawed there as well. The southern states were dependent on slave labor to operate their vast cotton plantations. If they had no slaves, they would face financial ruin.

Abraham Lincoln opposed slavery. Within days of his election as president in 1860, seven southern states broke away from the United States. Soon they were joined by four others. Virginia, Tennessee, Arkansas, Texas, Louisiana, Mississippi, Alabama, Georgia, Florida, North Carolina, and South Carolina formed a separate country, the Confederate States of America.[6]

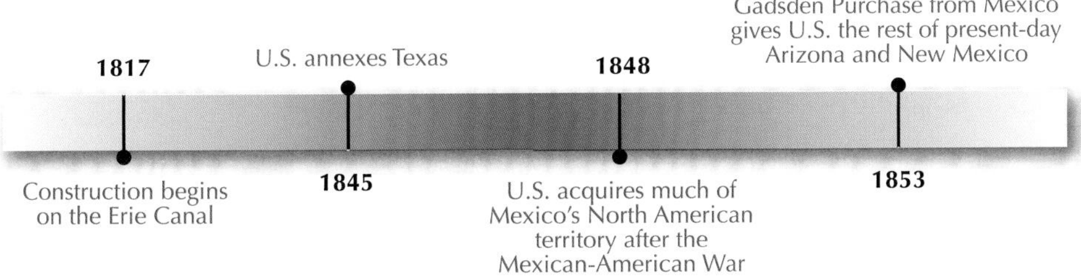
1817
Construction begins on the Erie Canal
1845
U.S. annexes Texas
1848
U.S. acquires much of Mexico's North American territory after the Mexican-American War
1853
Gadsden Purchase from Mexico gives U.S. the rest of present-day Arizona and New Mexico

Mexico City at the time of the Gadsden Purchase. In 1853 the United States bought part of southern Arizona and New Mexico from Mexico for 10 million dollars. These lands are still along the border between the two countries.

President Lincoln refused to let the country be divided. He meant to keep the southern states in the Union, by force if necessary. And force was necessary. The Confederates fired on Fort Sumter, a Union stronghold in South Carolina, in April 1861 and the Civil War was on.

For four years Americans fought against Americans, sometimes even brother against brother. The Civil War was one of the bloodiest wars in history. More than 600,000 men died. In the end, the Union prevailed. In April 1865 Confederate General Robert E. Lee surrendered to Union General Ulysses S. Grant at Appomattox, Virginia. Four

1861–1865
American Civil War is fought
Transcontinental railroad completed
1869
1914–1918
World War I is fought
Great Depression begins
1929
1939–1945
World War II is fought

days later President Lincoln was assassinated. The country was put back together, but its president was dead.[7]

After the war the United States worked to rebuild the south. Many southern cities were in ruins. Four million former slaves were now free.[8] They needed a way to earn a living for themselves and their families. Much work was to be done. This period was called Reconstruction. It was a difficult time.

By the end of the 1800s the United States had experienced enormous growth. Fifteen states had been added between 1850 and 1900.[9] Settlers continued surging over the western trails to settle in the new lands. The completion of the transcontinental railroad in 1869 spurred the westward rush. Thousands of white settlers poured into the "last frontier," the American West.

Since the abandonment of the Royal Proclamation line after the American Revolution, Indians had been pushed farther and farther west. Through treaties, purchases, and sometimes violence, white settlers moved in and Indians moved out. The great westward expansion created a final showdown between the two groups. Brutal conflicts between the United States Army and the Indians in the west lasted until the 1890s. By then the Indians had been overwhelmed by sheer numbers. They agreed to live on reservations, lands set aside for their use.

While many settlers moved to the western frontier, millions of immigrants from Europe arrived on the American east coast seeking a better way of life. The country's population grew from about 5 million in 1800 to more than 76 million in 1900.[10]

The twentieth century brought a new direction of growth and change for the United States. The vast resources of the west poured

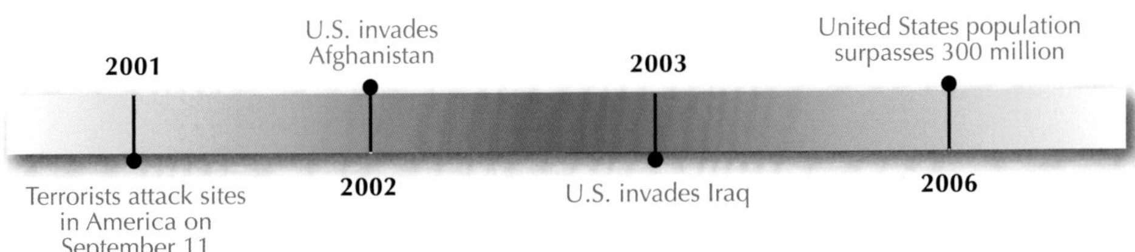
U.S. invades Afghanistan
United States population surpasses 300 million
2001
2003
Terrorists attack sites in America on September 11
2002
U.S. invades Iraq
2006

money into the economy. Lumber, gold, silver, iron ore and many other resources stimulated business and created jobs. New inventions for the home and workplace changed the way people worked. Machines performed jobs that humans used to do.

The United States was transformed from a small inexperienced country to a land of almost unlimited talents and resources. As it discovered its newfound powers, it changed the way it viewed itself and was viewed by other countries. Since the American Revolution, America had been an isolationist country. It stayed out of the affairs of other countries. The Spanish-American War in 1898 marked the emergence of the United States as a player in world politics as it acquired the Philippine Islands and other Spanish colonies. U.S. forces greatly influenced the outcome of World War I (1914–1918). The United States demonstrated that it would make a difference in the outcome of international events.

The American economy stumbled during the Great Depression, which began in 1929. Past mistakes in banking and business decisions led to many business and bank failures. Factories closed. People lost their jobs. Farmers lost their farms. The government, beginning with President Herbert Hoover and then President Franklin Roosevelt, passed laws to try to get the economy back on track. Some things worked, some did not.

In 1939, German leader Adolf Hitler invaded Poland to begin World War II. Great Britain and France were drawn into the war right away. The United States provided equipment and supplies but did not enter the war. That changed on December 7, 1941, when the Japanese bombed the American naval base at Pearl Harbor, Hawaii. The United States declared war immediately.

1861–1865
American Civil War is fought
Transcontinental railroad completed
1869
1914–1918
World War I is fought
Great Depression begins
1929
1939–1945
World War II is fought

Factories reopened to make weapons and other items for the war. Every available man and woman who was not in the military was needed to fill factory jobs. The economy flourished.

Scientists, too, contributed many new inventions, including one of the most fearsome weapons of all time: the atomic bomb. When the war ended in Europe in May 1945, President Harry Truman gave the order to use atomic weapons on two cities in Japan a few months later to hasten the end of the war in Asia.

Smoke billows around U.S. battleships hit by Japanese aircraft during the December 7, 1941, attack on Pearl Harbor.

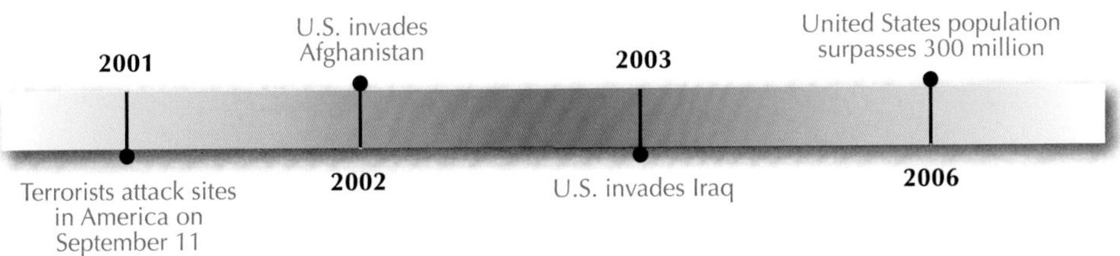
2001
Terrorists attack sites in America on September 11
U.S. invades Afghanistan
2002
2003
U.S. invades Iraq
United States population surpasses 300 million
2006

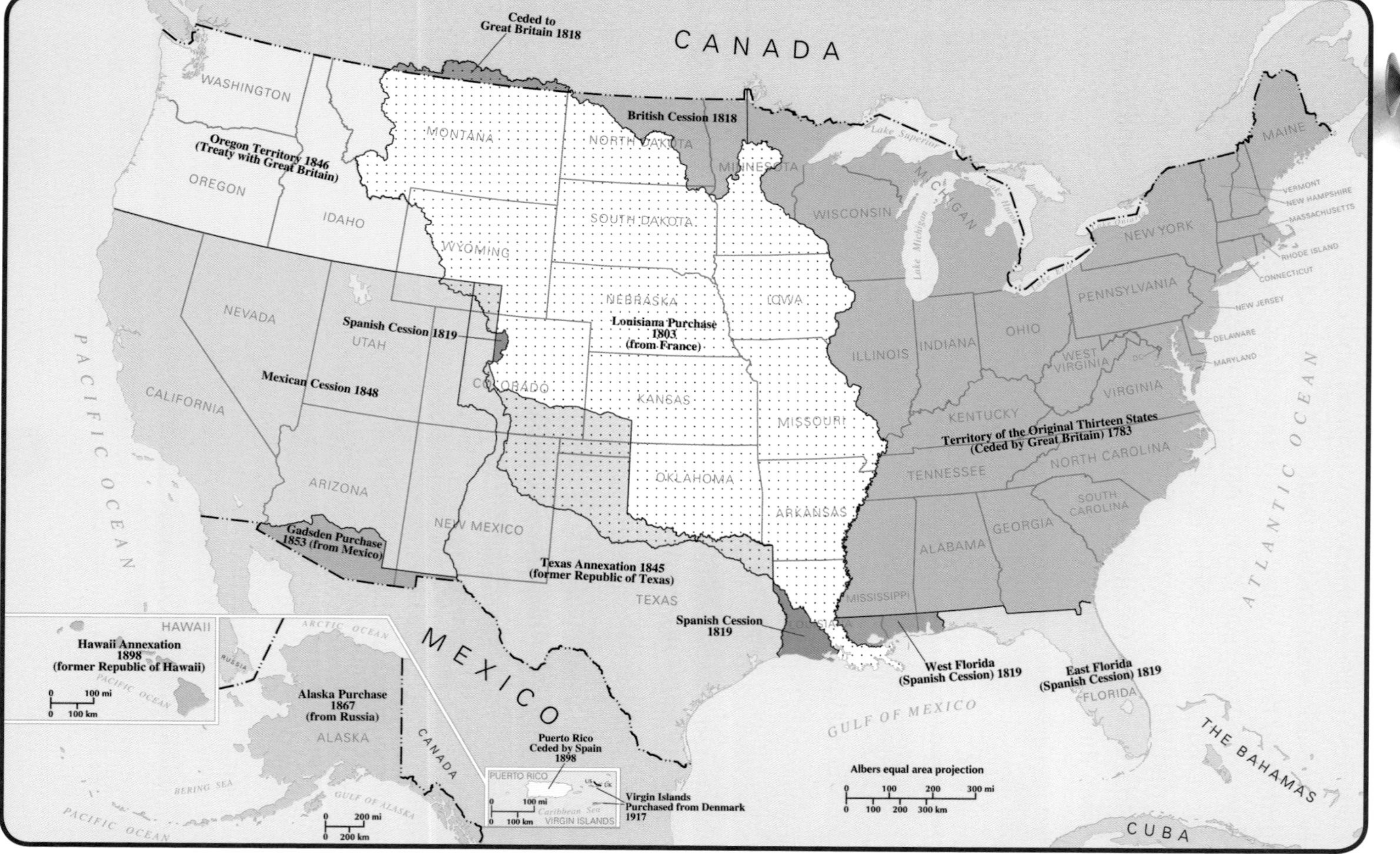

By the mid-1800s the United States had acquired most of its present territory. Many western lands were years from statehood, but the groundwork had been laid. The country did indeed stretch “from sea to shining sea.”

After World War II all the old superpowers of the past (England, France, Germany, Spain) had been surpassed by the United States and the Soviet Union. The two remaining superpowers had the right combination of natural resources and political leadership to move them ahead in the world order.

The two countries found themselves rivals over political and military issues. The Soviet Union was a communist country with strict control over its people and their activities. The United States was a democracy with leaders elected by its citizens and laws created by elected officials. Both countries had advanced industrial and scientific resources. Both had nuclear weapons. From the 1950s each feared a nuclear attack from the other. This period was known as the Cold War. The Cold War ended with the collapse of the Soviet Union in 1991.

As the world's remaining superpower, the United States had many benefits to offer its citizens. But it also became a target for enemies. Terrorist attacks occurred in the 1990s at American sites around the world as well as on American soil. The terrorist attacks in New York City and Washington, D.C., on September 11, 2001, killed nearly three thousand people and was the impetus for the invasion of Afghanistan in 2002 and Iraq the following year.

Once ragtag groups of shelters around wooden stockades on the Delaware and Hudson Rivers, the former colonies of New Sweden and New Netherland were swallowed up by events around them. They were taken over by the English in the seventeenth century, swallowed by the American colonies, and then became states after the American Revolution. As part of the United States of America, these tiny colonies are now part of the world's only remaining superpower. Where

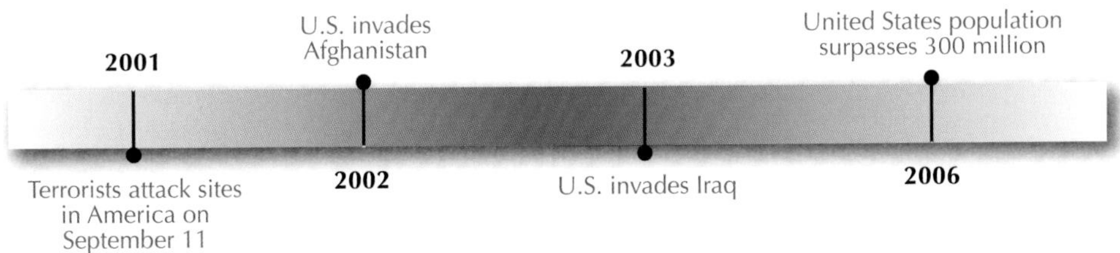
2001
Terrorists attack sites in America on September 11
U.S. invades Afghanistan
2002
2003
U.S. invades Iraq
United States population surpasses 300 million
2006

"All the News That's Fit to Print"

The New York Times

Late Edition

VOL. CL . . . No. 51,874 — NEW YORK, WEDNESDAY, SEPTEMBER 12, 2001 — 75 CENTS

U.S. ATTACKED

HIJACKED JETS DESTROY TWIN TOWERS AND HIT PENTAGON IN DAY OF TERROR

A CREEPING HORROR

Buildings Burn and Fall as Onlookers Search for Elusive Safety

President Vows to Exact Punishment for 'Evil'

A Somber Bush Says Terrorism Cannot Prevail

Awaiting the Aftershocks

Washington and Nation Plunge Into Fight With Enemy Hard to Identify and Punish

MORE ON THE ATTACKS

Terrorists shocked the world with multiple attacks on United States targets on September 11, 2001. Thousands of Americans died in the attacks, led by members of an Islamic group known as al-Qaeda. Many world leaders immediately condemned their actions.

once gruff and bearded traders hauled beaver skins through the wilderness, highways, shopping malls, and cities sprawl across the landscape. Billions of dollars' worth of transactions occur every day where a day's work was once paid for with a handful of shells. From such humble beginnings has risen one of the greatest industrial nations the world has ever known.

Where Are They Now?

New France, New Netherland, and New Sweden no longer exist, but many clues to their existence remain.

Perhaps the most obvious evidence of New France is the French language itself. Canada has two official languages: French and English. Many people in Canada speak both.

The explorers and voyageurs spread far and wide over the North American continent. Many of the places they named still exist today. For example, Detroit, in Michigan, takes its name from the French word for "strait," a narrow body of water. There it refers to the narrow waterway between Lake Huron and Lake Erie. Lake Champlain in upstate New York is named for Samuel de Champlain. The adjacent state of Vermont takes its name from the French words for "green mountains."

Traces of New Netherland are everywhere in the New York City area.

- Long Island—*Lang Eylant*, literally "long island"
- Staten Island—*Staten Eylant*, named for the Dutch governing body, the States General
- Brooklyn—named for the Dutch city of Breuckelen
- Harlem—named for the Dutch city of Haarlem
- Greenwich Village—originally Greenwyck ("pine district")
- The Bronx—originally Jonas Bronck's plantation

It's not just place names. The Dutch introduced the St. Nicholas/Santa Claus legend to America. In 1915, the city of New York incorporated the orange, blue, and white colors of the Dutch flag into the city's official flag. These colors appear today in the uniforms of the New York Mets baseball team and New York Knicks basketball team.[11]

New Sweden left behind place names such as the Christina River and Swedesboro, New Jersey. Churches, parks and historical sites with Swedish connections are plentiful on both sides of Delaware Bay.

The first Swedish settlers arrived on two ships, the *Kalmar Nyckel* and the *Fogel Grip*. In the 1990s volunteers raised money to build a full-sized replica of the *Kalmar Nyckel*.[12] The Kalmar Nyckel Foundation regularly invites the public onboard for deck tours and sailing experiences along the Eastern Seaboard.

The replica of the *Kalmar Nyckel* can still be seen today sailing along the Delaware River.

1524 Giovanni da Verrazzano explores North American coast for France

1529 *Gallia Nova* (New France) first appears on a map, which is prepared by a brother of Verrazzano

1534 Jacques Cartier claims New France for King Francis I and enters the St. Lawrence River

1542 French colony fails but fur trade initiated

1603 Samuel de Champlain sails up St. Lawrence River

1608 Champlain founds Quebec

1609 Henry Hudson explores New York Harbor and Hudson River

1615 Champlain is shown route to Great Lakes

1624 Dutch found New Netherland

1626 Peter Minuit purchases Manhattan Island for the Dutch

1627 Cardinal Richelieu founds Company of New France / Company of the Hundred Associates to encouragement settlement in New France

1628 English intercept French supply fleet bound for Quebec; Champlain forced to surrender and return to France

1632 Minuit is replaced as governor of New Netherland

1638 Minuit founds Swedish colony on Delaware River

1642 French Catholic Church founds Montreal

1647 Peter Stuyvesant is named governor of New Netherland

1653 New Amsterdam citizens construct wall at north end of city; path next to the wall becomes known as Wall Street, which eventually becomes center of U.S. financial industry

1654 Swedes take Dutch Fort Casimir

1655 Stuyvesant retakes New Sweden

1664 New Amsterdam's captured by English and renamed New York after James, Duke of York, brother of King Charles II

1665 French begin campaign against Iroquois

1673 Louis Joliet and Jacques Marquette become first French to see Mississippi River

Timeline

1681	King Charles II gives area including former New Sweden to William Penn
1682	Robert de La Salle claims Ohio and Mississippi valleys as far as Gulf of Mexico for France
1685	James, Duke of York, becomes King of England
1699	Louisiana is founded by the French
1702	Queen Anne's War/War of Spanish Succession begins
1718	New Orleans is founded
1754	French and Indian War begins
1760	British defeat French in Canada
1763	Treaty of Paris cedes almost all of New France outside of New Orleans to Britain
1775–1783	American Revolution
1783	North West Company is founded
1787	U.S. Congress passes Northwest Ordinance, dictating how new territories will be added
1791	Constitutional Act (Canada Act) divides Canada into Upper Canada and Lower Canada
1803	U.S. President Thomas Jefferson concludes Louisiana Purchase from France
1812	War of 1812 begins
1814	Treaty of Ghent ends War of 1812, establishes border between U.S. and Canada
1821	North West Company merges with Hudson's Bay Company
1837	Rebellions in Upper and Lower Canada flare against the British
1840	Union Act unites Upper and Lower Canada into Province of Canada
1845	United States annexes Texas
1846	Oregon boundary settled at 49th parallel
1848	U.S. acquires much of Mexico's North American territory after the Mexican-American War
1853	United States acquires the rest of present-day Arizona and New Mexico through the Gadsden Purchase
1858	Fraser River Gold Rush begins

Timeline

1867	British North American Act unites Province of Canada, New Brunswick, and Nova Scotia as Dominion of Canada
1869	Transcontinental railroad is completed at Promontory Point Utah; Dominion of Canada acquires Rupert's Land, sparking the Red River Rebellion
1870	Manitoba joins Dominion of Canada
1871	British Columbia becomes Canada's sixth province
1873	Prince Edward Island joins Dominion of Canada
1885	Canada Pacific Railway is completed
1898	Yukon Territory is established
1905	Saskatchewan and Alberta join Canada
1914–1918	World War I
1929	Great Depression begins in the United States and Canada
1939–1945	World War II
1949	Newfoundland becomes Canada's tenth province
1997	Replica of the *Kalmar Nyckel* is built in Wilmington, Delaware
1999	Territory of Nunavut is established
2001	Newfoundland is renamed Newfoundland and Labrador; Terrorists attack World Trade Center in Manhattan and the Pentagon in Washington, D.C.
2002	United States invades Afghanistan
2003	United States invades Iraq
2005	Canada's population passes 32 million; Mexico's population is about 105 million
2006	United States' population surpasses 300 million
2007	Royal Canadian Mounted Police Heritage Center opens in Regina, Saskatchewan

Chapter Notes

Chapter 1. Beads and Hatchets

1. Russell Shorto, *The Island at the Center of the World: The Epic Story of Dutch Manhattan and the Forgotten Colony that Shaped America* (New York: Doubleday, 2004), p. 50.

2. Ibid., p. 42.

3. Ibid., p. 46.

4. Robert S. Grumet, *The Lenapes* (New York: Chelsea House Publishers, 1989), p. 16; C. A. Weslager, *New Sweden on the Delaware 1638–1655* (Wilmington, Delaware: The Middle Atlantic Press, 1988), p. 44.

5. Grumet, p. 16; Weslager, pp. 43–44.

6. Tara Prindle, "Wampum History and Background," *Nativetech: Native American Technology and Art*, http://www.nativetech.org/wampum/wamphist.htm.

7. Louis Jordan, "Wampum: Introduction," *The Coins of Colonial and Early America*, http://www.coins.nd.edu/colcoinintros/wampum.intro.html; Prindle.

8. Prindle.

9. Jordan.

Chapter 2. New France, 1534–1763

1. Wolfgang Schivelbusch, "Spices, or the Dawn of the Modern Age," from *Tastes of Paradise: A Social History of Spices, Stimulants and Intoxicants* as excerpted at *The Epicentre* website, http://www.theepicentre.com/Spices/excerpt2.html.

2. W. J. Eccles, *The French in North America 1500–1783* (Markham, Ontario: Fitzhenry Whiteside, 1998), pp. 1–2; Samuel Eliot Morison, *Samuel Champlain: Father of New France* (Boston: Atlantic Monthly Press, 1972), p. 4.

3. Eccles, p. 2; Morison, p. 3; Andre Vachon, *Dreams of Empire: Canada Before 1700* (Ottawa: Canadian Government Publishing Center, 1982), p. 3.

4. Craig Brown, "Jacques Cartier: New Land for the French King," *The Illustrated History of Canada*, http://www.collectionscanada.ca/explorers/kids/h3-1320-e.html.

5. Morison, p. 23; Vachon, p. 3.

6. Morison, p. 24.

7. Eccles, p. 12.

8. Ken Mitchell, "The Beaver Fur Trade," *James Ford Bell Library*, www.bell.lib.umn.edu/products/beaver.html

9. Eccles, p. 13; Ted Morgan, *Wilderness at Dawn: The Settling of the North American Continent* (New York: Simon & Schuster, 1993,) p. 91.; Morison, pp. 3, 36; Vachon, p. 4.

10. Morgan, pp. 92, 94; Morison, p. 102; Vachon, pp. 3–4.

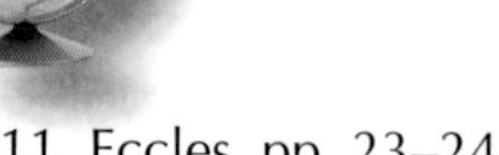

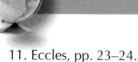

11. Eccles, pp. 23–24.

12. Morison, pp. 192, 195; Marcel Trudel, "Samuel de Champlain," *Dictionary of Canadian Biographies Online*, http://www.biographi.ca/EN/ShowBio.asp?BioId=34237; Vachon, p. 5.

13. Eccles, pp. 32–33; Trudel.

14. Morgan, p. 100.

15. Eccles p. 99; Andre Vachon, "Louis Joliet," *Dictionary of Canadian Biographies Online*, http://www.biographi.ca/EN/ShowBio.asp?BioId=34427&query=jolliet.

16. Eccles, p. 85.

17. Ibid., p. 119.

18. Ibid., pp. 192, 198, 203, 233.

19. France retained fishing rights off Newfoundland and a few scattered islands there and in the Caribbean; Eccles p. 238.

20. Robert S. Grumet, *The Lenapes* (New York: Chelsea House Publishers, 1989), p. 43; "The Beaver," Canadian Heritage, http://www.pch.gc.ca/progs/cpsc-ccsp/sc-cs/o1_e.cfm.

21. "The Beaver," Canadian Heritage.

Chapter 3. New Netherland, 1624–1664

1. C. R. Boxer, *The Dutch Seaborne Empire: 1600–1800* (New York: Alfred A. Knopf, 1970), p. 3; Russell Shorto, *The Island at the Center of the World: The Epic Story of Dutch Manhattan and the Forgotten Colony That Shaped America* (New York: Doubleday, 2004), pp. 23–31.

2. Shorto, p. 31.

3. Ibid., pp. 31–34.

4. Ibid., p. 34.

5. Ibid., pp. 37, 41–46.

6. Ibid., pp. 49–50.

7. Ibid., p. 61.

8. Ibid., pp. 65, 71, 75.

9. Ibid., p. 65.

10. Ibid., p.105.

11. Ibid., p. 28.

12. Ibid., pp. 117–118, 121–122.

13. Ibid., pp. 127, 167.

14. Ibid., p. 147.

15. Ibid., pp. 216, 249.

16. Ibid., pp. 277–279.

17. Ibid., pp. 285–286, 294.

18. Ibid., pp. 295–296.
19. Robert S. Grumet, *The Lenapes* (New York: Chelsea House Publishers, 1989), pp. 13, 35.
20. Grumet, p. 16; Weslager, pp. 42–44.
21. Ibid.
22. Weslager, p. 46.
23. Edwin G. Burrows and Mike Wallace, *Gotham: A History of New York to 1898* (New York: Oxford University Press, 1999), pp. 37–38.
24. Grumet, p. 95; Weslager, p. 207.

Chapter 4. New Sweden, 1638–1655

1. C. A. Weslager, *New Sweden on the Delaware 1638–1655* (Wilmington, Delaware: The Middle Atlantic Press, 1988), pp. 12, 20.
2. Ibid., pp. 20–21.
3. Ibid., pp. 31, 36, 39.
4. Ibid., p. 136.
5. Ibid., pp. 49–50.
6. Ibid., pp. 52–54.
7. Ibid., pp. 59–60.
8. Ibid., pp. 62, 69–70, 90–91.
9. Ibid., p. 119.
10. Ibid., pp. 121–124.
11. Ibid., pp. 125–126.
12. Ibid., p. 127.
13. Ibid., p. 126.
14. Ibid., pp. 129–132.
15. Ibid., pp. 134–135.
16. Ibid., p. 145.
17. Ibid., pp. 164–170.
18. Russell Shorto, *The Island at the Center of the World: The Epic Story of Dutch Manhattan and the Forgotten Colony That Shaped America* (New York: Doubleday, 2004), pp. 48, 65, 88; Weslager, pp. 22–24, 34–35, 51.

Chapter 5. Canada 1763–1867

1. Scott W. See, *The History of Canada* (Westport, Connecticut: Greenwood Press, 2001), p. 55.
2. Ibid., p. 59.
3. Gerald S. Graham, *A Concise History of Canada* (New York: The Viking Press, 1968), p. 96; W. Kaye Lamb, *The History of Canada From Discovery to Present Day* (New York: American Heritage Press, 1971), p. 69; See, p. 60.

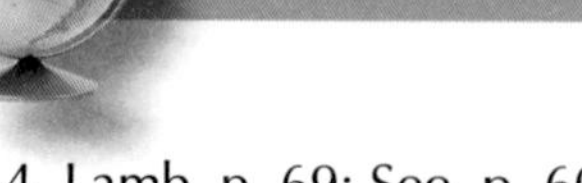

4. Lamb, p. 69; See, p. 60.

5. Lamb, pp. 70–71.

6. Desmond Morton, *A Short History of Canada* (Edmonton: Hurtig Publishers Ltd., 1983), p. 21; See, p. 62; Lamb, p. 86; Graham, p. 99.

7. Graham, p. 102; Lamb, p. 88; Morton, p. 24; See, p. 63.

8. Lamb, p. 101; See, pp. 63–64.

9. Margaret Conrad, Alfin Finkel, and Veronica Strong-Boag, *History of the Canadian Peoples, Beginnings to 1867. Volume I.* (Toronto: Addison, Wesley, Longman, 2002), p. 409; Graham, p. 130.

10. B. Griffin, "Fraser River Gold Rush," *Royal British Columbia Museum*, http://www.em.gov.bc.ca/mining/geolsurv/publications/openfiles/of1992019/goldrush.html; Graham, p. 136.

Chapter 6. Canada, 1867–Present

1. Gerald S. Graham, *A Concise History of Canada* (New York: The Viking Press, 1968), p. 133; Desmond Morton, *A Short History of Canada* (Edmonton, Alberta: Hurtig Publishers Ltd., 1983), p. 9.

2. J. M. Bumsted, *A History of the Canadian Peoples* (Toronto: Oxford University Press, 1998), p. 187.

3. *Manitoba Cultural Heritage*, http://www.gov.mb.ca/chc/hrb/plaques/plaq0945.html

4. Morton, p. 121.

5. Scott W. See, *The History of Canada* (Westport, Connecticut: Greenwood Press, 2001), p. 101.

6. W. Kaye Lamb, *The History of Canada From Discovery to Present Day* (New York: American Heritage Press, 1971), p. 238.

7. Morton, p. 179; See, p. 121.

8. Bumsted, pp. 187, 208; See, pp. 92, 101.

9. Lamb, p. 295; See, p. 143

10. See, p. 192.

11. George Woodcock, *The Canadians* (Cambridge, Massachusetts: Harvard University Press, 1979), p. 230.

12. "Wheat," *Canadian Encyclopedia*, http://www.canadianencyclopedia.ca

13. "The Beaver," *Canadian Heritage*, http://www.pch.gc.ca/progs/cpsc-ccsp/sc-cs/o1_e.cfm

14. *Royal Canadian Mounted Police*, http://www.rcmp.ca/index_e.htm

Chapter Notes

Chapter 7. United States, 1664–1783

1. *State of Delaware*, http://www.state.de.us/gic/facts/history/delhist.shtml; Carol E. Hoffecker, *Delaware: A Bicentennial History* (New York: W.W. Norton and Sons, 1977), p. 159.
2. *State of Delaware*.
3. *Liberty! The American Revolution*, http://www.pbs.org/ktca/liberty/chronicle_boston1774.html
4. *State of Delaware*; Hoffecker, p. 159.
5. Hoffecker, pp. 160, 167.
6. *Heritage New York*, http://www.heritageny.gov/RevWar/revwar.cfm
7. Edwin G. Burrows and Mike Wallace, *Gotham: A History of New York to 1898* (New York: Oxford University Press, 1999), pp. 219, 235.
8. Burrows, p. 169.

Chapter 8. United States, 1783–Present

1. Robert Kelley, *The Shaping of the American Past, Second Edition* (Englewood Cliffs, New Jersey: Prentice-Hall, Inc., 1978), pp. 106–107.
2. Alan Axelrod and Charles Phillips, *What Every American Should Know About American History: 200 Events That Shaped the Nation* (Holbrook, Massachusetts: Adams Media Corporation, 1992), p. 80; Kelley, p. 146.
3. Kelley, p. 151.
4. Kelley, p. 185; Russell Shorto, *The Island at the Center of the World: The Epic Story of Dutch Manhattan and the Forgotten Colony that Shaped America* (New York: Doubleday, 2004), pp. 316–317.
5. Kelley, pp. 257–258.
6. Ibid., p. 341.
7. Ibid., pp. 348, 369.
8. Ibid., p. 374.
9. California, Minnesota, Oregon, Kansas, West Virginia, Nevada, Nebraska, Colorado, North Dakota, South Dakota, Montana, Washington, Idaho, Wyoming, Utah.
10. 1900 data from U.S. Census Bureau, http://www.census.gov/rochi/www/fun1.html.
11. Shorto, pp. 183fn, 314–315, map on frontispiece.
12. *Kalmar Nyckel*, http://www.kalmarnyckel.org.

Books

Boraas, Tacey. *Canada.* Mankato, Minnesota: Capstone Press, 2002.

Faber, Harold. *Samuel Champlain: Explorer of Canada.* New York: Benchmark Books, 2004.

Harmon, Daniel E. *The Early French Explorers of North America.* Broomall, Pennsylvania: Mason Crest Publishers, 2002.

Heinrichs, Ann. *The Netherlands.* New York: Children's Press, 2003.

King, David C. *First Facts About U.S. History.* Woodbridge, Connecticut: Blackbirch Press, 1996.

Riehecky, Janet. *Sweden.* Mankato, Minnesota: Capstone Press, 2006.

Wiener, Roberta, and James R. Arnold. *New York: The History of New York Colony, 1624–1776.* Austin, Texas: Raintree, 2004.

Works Consulted

Anderson, Fred. *The War That Made America: A Short History of the French and Indian War.* New York: Viking, 2005.

Axelrod, Alan, and Charles Phillips. *What Every American Should Know About American History.* Holbrook, Massachusetts: Adams Media Corporation, 1992.

Boxer, C. R. *The Dutch Seaborne Empire: 1600–1800.* New York: Alfred A. Knopf, 1970.

Brown, Craig. *The Illustrated History of Canada:* "Jacques Cartier: New Land for the French King," http://www.collectionscanada.ca/explorers/kids/h3-1320-e.html

Bumsted, J. M. *A History of the Canadian Peoples.* Toronto: Oxford University Press, 1998.

Burrows, Edwin G., and Mike Wallace. *Gotham: A History of New York to 1898.* New York: Oxford University Press, 1999.

Canadian Encyclopedia: "Wheat" http://www.canadianencyclopedia.ca/index.cfm?PgNm=TCE&Params=A1ARTA0008543

Canadian Heritage: "The Beaver," http://www.pch.gc.ca/progs/cpsc-ccsp/sc-cs/o1_e.cfm

Conrad, Margaret, and Alfin Finkel. *History of the Canadian Peoples, Beginnings to 1867.* Volume I. 3rd ed. Toronto: Addison Wesley Longman, 2002.

Conrad, Margaret, Alfin Finkel, and Veronica Strong-Boag. *History of the Canadian Peoples, 1867 to the Present.* Volume II. Toronto: Copp Clark Pitman Ltd., 1993.

Eccles, W. J. *The French in North America 1500–1783.* East Lansing: Michigan State University Press, 1998.

Further Reading

Graham, Gerald S. *A Concise History of Canada*. New York: The Viking Press, 1968.

Griffin, B. British Columbia Government: "Miners at Work, A History of British Columbia's Gold Rushes," http://www.em.gov.bc.ca/Mining/Geolsurv/Publications/OpenFiles/OF1992-19/GoldRush.html

Grumet, Robert S. *The Lenapes*. New York: Chelsea House Publishers, 1989.

Hamelin, Jean. *Dictionary of Canadian Biographies Online:* "Jean Nicolett de Bellborne," http://www.biographi.ca/EN/ShowBio.asp?BioId=34552&query=nicollet

Heritage New York, "Revolutionary War in New York," http://www.heritageny.gov/RevWar/rwny.cfm

Hoffecker, Carol E. *Delaware: A Bicentennial History*. New York: W.W. Norton and Sons, 1977.

Jordan, Louis. *The Coins of Colonial and Early America:* "Wampum: Introduction," http://www.coins.nd.edu/ColCoin/ColCoinIntros/Wampum.intro.html

Kelley, Robert. *The Shaping of the American Past*. 2nd ed. Englewood Cliffs, New Jersey: Prentice-Hall, Inc., 1978.

Lamb, W. Kaye. *The History of Canada From Discovery to Present Day*. New York: American Heritage Press, 1971.

Liberty! Chronicle of the American Revolution: "Boston 1774," http://www.pbs.org/ktca/liberty/chronicle_boston1774.html

Maier, Pauline. *Inventing America*. New York: W.W. Norton, 2003.

Manitoba Cultural Heritage, "Manitoba Heritage Council Commemorative Plaques," http://www.gov.mb.ca/chc/hrb/plaques/plaq0945.html

Mitchell, Ken. James Ford Bell Library: "The Beaver Fur Trade," http://bell.lib.umn.edu/Products/beaver.html

Morgan, Ted. *Wilderness at Dawn: The Settling of the North American Continent*. New York: Simon & Schuster, 1993.

Morison, Samuel E. *Samuel Champlain: Father of New France*. Boston: Atlantic Monthly Press, 1972.

Morton, Desmond. *A Short History of Canada*. Edmonton: Hurtig Publishers Ltd., 1983.

Prindle, Tara. *Nativetech: Native American Technology and Art:* "Wampum History and Background," http://www.nativetech.org/wampum/wamphist.htm

Riendeau, Roger. *A Brief History of Canada*. New York: Facts on File, 2000.

Royal Canadian Mounted Police, http://www.rcmp.ca/index_e.htm

Schivelbusch, Wolfgang. The Epicentre: "Spices, or the Dawn of the Modern Age" excerpted from *Tastes of Paradise: A Social History of Spices,*

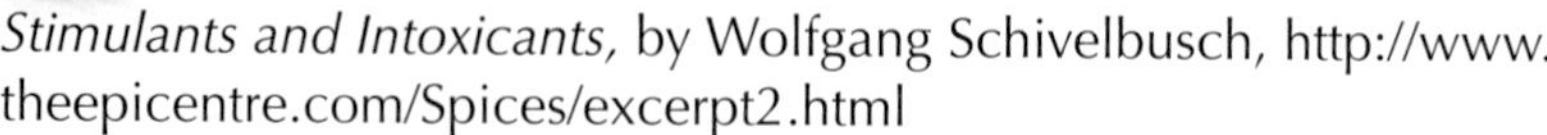

Stimulants and Intoxicants, by Wolfgang Schivelbusch, http://www.theepicentre.com/Spices/excerpt2.html

See, Scott W. *The History of Canada*. Westport, Connecticut: Greenwood Press, 2001.

Shorto, Russell. *The Island at the Center of the World: The Epic Story of Dutch Manhattan and the Forgotten Colony That Shaped America.* New York: Doubleday, 2004.

State of Delaware. "A Brief History," http://www.state.de.us/gic/facts/history/delhist.shtml

Trudel, Marcel. *Dictionary of Canadian Biographies Online:* "Samuel de Champlain," http://www.biographi.ca/EN/ShowBio.asp?BioId=34237

United States Census Bureau, http://www.census.gov/

Vachon, André. *Dictionary of Canadian Biographies Online:* "Louis Jolliet," http://www.biographi.ca/EN/ShowBio.asp?BioId=34427&query=jolliet

Vachon, André. *Dreams of Empire: Canada Before 1700.* Ottawa: Canadian Government Publishing Center, 1982.

Weslager, C. A. *New Sweden on the Delaware 1638–1655.* Wilmington, Delaware: The Middle Atlantic Press, 1988.

Woodcock, George. *The Canadians.* Cambridge, Massachusetts: Harvard University Press, 1979.

On The Internet

The Canadian Encyclopedia
www.thecanadianencyclopedia.com

Dictionary of Canadian Biography Online
http://www.biographi.ca/

Heritage New York, "Revolutionary War Heritage Trail"
http://www.heritageny.gov/RevWar/revwar.cfm

Kalmar Nyckel
www.kalmarnyckel.org

Library and Archives Canada
http://www.collectionscanada.ca/index-e.html

New York State Facts
http://www.dos.state.ny.us/kidsroom/nysfacts/hstry1.html

PBS: The War That Made America (French and Indian War)
http://www.pbs.org/thewarthatmadeamerica/index.html

Royal Canadian Mounted Police
http://www.rcmp.ca/index_e.htm

The Swedish Colonial Society, "A Brief History of New Sweden in America"
http://www.colonialswedes.org/History/History.html

Glossary

colony (KAH-luh-nee)—an area settled or governed by a separate, distant power.

confederacy (kun-FEH-der-uh-see)—a term used to define the southern states that broke away during the American Civil War.

currency (KER-in-see)—something used as money.

democracy (duh-MAH-kruh-see)—system of government in which the people elect their leaders and are treated fairly by their government.

epidemic (eh-puh-DEH-mik)—a disease affecting many people at the same time.

flotilla (flow-TIL-uh)—a group of ships.

hordes (hordz)—a large group of people; a crowd.

impetus (IM-peh-tuss)—reason or motivation; force.

landlocked (LAND-lokt)—completely or almost completely surrounded by land, with no access to the sea.

militia (muh-LIH-shuh)—citizens trained to use weapons in times of emergency.

quartz (kwarts)—a common mineral found in many different types of rocks.

ragtag (RAG-tag)—made up of many different types.

scurvy (SKER-vee)—a disease resulting from a lack of vitamin C in the diet.

sieur (syuhr)—sir; a title of respect used by the French.

slavery (SLAY-ver-ee)—owning humans as property, usually for the purpose of having them work for no pay.

sluice (SLOO-iss)—an aluminum or steel box used to sift gold.

tax (taks)—a fee charged by governments to help pay for its services.

terrorist (TER-er-ist)—individuals who use extreme tactics against others in order to frighten them to do what the terrorist wants.

transaction (tranz-AK-shun)—an exchange of goods, services, or money between individuals or groups.

treaty (TREE-tee)—an agreement between two or more states or countries.

union (YOON-yun)—the northern states that were united during the American Civil War.

valiantly (VAL-yent-lee)—showing bravery.

Index

Index

Index

About the Author

Lissa Johnston

Think history is boring? So did author Lissa Johnston—until she took a history class in college that was actually interesting, entertaining, and fun! She switched majors, earned a master's degree in history, and has been thinking, reading, and writing about history ever since.

Lissa is a member of the Society of Children's Book Writers and Illustrators. She has written books in a variety of genres including biographies, social studies, and historical fiction. She also enjoys speaking to students at conferences and on school visits.

Born in Alpine, Texas, Lissa grew up in Dallas. She now lives in Fort Mill, South Carolina, with her husband, two children, and a yellow lab named Chloe. When she is not writing, Lissa enjoys reading, computing, playing tennis, and eating Mexican food.